Lessons from the Martial Arts

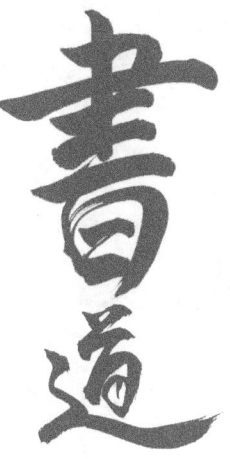

Shōdo

Brush Calligraphy

From Simple Fun to True Self-Mastery

Techniques and Exercises for Beginners

Dr. Jonathan Bannister, Ph.D./M.D.Sc.
AiShinKai Founder and President

AiShinKai Publications
Self-Mastery in Daily Life
www.aishinkai.com

Publisher
AiShinKai **Publications**
a division of **AiShinKai**, LLC
18201 76th Avenue West
Edmonds, WA 98026 USA
tel. 425-771-6816
www.aishinkai.com

ISBN-13   978-0615434629 (AiShinKai Publications)

ISBN-10   0615434622

First edition 2011

Contents

Shodo Brush Calligraphy
From Simple Fun to True Self-Mastery

Dr. Jonathan Bannister, Ph.D./Ma.D.Sc.
AiShinKai Founder and President

Forward	**5**
Introduction: The Case for Calmness	**7**

Part 1 - From Simple Fun to True Self-Mastery — **11**

The Tools of Brush Calligraphy: "Four Treasures"	17
Brushing Your Way to Leadership Skills	18
AiShinKai Breathing and Meditation Exercises	24
Basic Principles of Shodo	25
The Martial Arts Experience: Brush and Sword are One	28
Shodo and the Martial Arts	34
The Discovery of Self-Mastery	36

Part 2 - Practice Samples — **39**

The Twelve Basic Strokes of Shodo Brush Calligraphy	41
Horizontal Lines	42
Vertical Lines	43
Basic Stroke Work Sheets	45
Single Kanji	59
Kakejiku: Scroll Arrangements	69
Four-Character Idioms	81
Blank Worksheet	87
Good for Kids Too . . . (Kanji Worksheet)	89

Part 3 - Study Examples — **91**

References, Bibliography, Resources	**105**
Shodo Terminology	**107**
Kanji List	**108**
Index	**122**

Shodo Brush Calligraphy
From Simple Fun to True Self-Mastery

Dr. Jonathan Bannister, Ph.D./Ma.D.Sc.
AiShinKai Founder and President

Shodo brush calligraphy is incorporated into every program taught at *AiShinKai*, an organization dedicated to the cultivation self-mastery through the study of Japanese martial and traditional cultural arts. Brushing Chinese and Japanese characters is the basis of an accessible, playful and rich art, the "way of writing beautifully." Formal in its principles and rules, Shodo encourages expression of personal freedom and dynamicism once certain rules are mastered. Everyone who engages in the discipline learns a great deal about themselves and the world: it is the greatest thing since finger-painting to promote self-discovery. Scholars, rulers, generals, and priests from ancient China and Japan highly valued calligraphy skill. A person was not considered educated unless he could brush with authority. Much more than mere writing, the discipline was understood as a means to cultivate the Self. Even in modern Japan, an absence of brush calligraphy skill exposes a tremendous hole an individual's education that is difficult to fill by other means. Aside from that, Shodo remains a fun and engaging art that can be enjoyed by all.

This book began life as a series of worksheets and essays, and retains some of that character. It is an introduction to the principles and the art as it relates to AiShinKai self-mastery training. I hope that readers will experience the marvelously sensuous pleasure of brush and ink applied to paper, and will also discover new tools for developing a unified mind and body, and for experiencing the profound sense of calmness at the heart of "a life worth living."

I wish to express deep appreciation to the teachers and friends who have encouraged my interest in Japanese martial and cultural arts. Maruyama Shuji Sensei of Kokikai International, the late Don Yoshimoto Trent Sensei of Tsubomi Seishin Kan Iaido Kai in Tokyo, and Eura Kazunori Sensei (All Japan Kendo Federation Iaido *hachidan hanshi*) of the *Hajime Kai* in Tokyo have all helped me on the path to self-mastery. Special mention should be made of Mr. Koyama Kunihisa, Aikido instructor in Tokyo, Japan, my good friend Keith Cullen, and Lee Jamison of TLC in Shoreline, WA. I appreciate the support of the **Pacific Northwest Budo Association** and my friends, students, and co-instructors at AiShinKai. Thanks to Kowaji-san, owner of *Sora* Japanese restaurant in Tachikawa, and Mr. Suga and Usami Yui, who help me to remain calm and happy when I visit the wonderful country of Japan. Finally, great and abiding love to my wife Wendy, son Kelsey, and mother Karen Bannister, whose unfailing graciousness, generosity, and artistic example is a continual inspiration.

March 2011

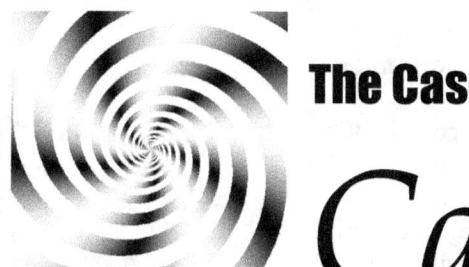

The Case for

Calmness

The cultivation of calmness lies at the root of AiShinKai self-mastery training. Whether one paints with a brush, exercises leadership in business or civil service, or trains to achieve peak performance in a sport or martial discipline, the ability to perceive, think and act with dependable calmness is an important key to success. Originally published in The Path to Self-Mastery: Lessons from the Martial Arts to Achieve Peak Performance in Business, Sports, and Daily Life (**AiShinKai** Publications 2011)

*M*aybe I need new glasses. I have a headache after writing for several hours, and it's getting harder to read the finely printed instructions on frozen pizza boxes (for my son, honest!). Any experience of internal discord is like needing glasses. When we're upset, psycho-chemical factors come into play that limit vision, create tension, and inhibit rationality. We cease being able to perceive conditions and situations clearly. Even a slight feeling of ill-ease will cause the brain react as if it were viewing the world through coke bottle lenses. This interferes with problem analysis and resolution. The cultivation of a dependable sense of calmness is essential to effective performance in every aspect of life.

As an educator, business leader, and Japanese martial and cultural artist, I rely on a profound sense of calmness cultivated during more than four decades of rigorous

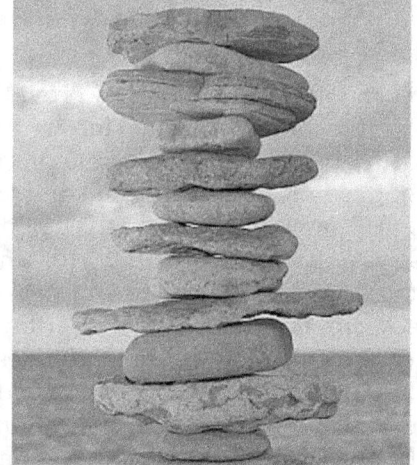

movement training. Calmness helps me to listen more clearly: a quality essential in all relationships. It allows me to respond to what is actually meant, rather than what is merely said. Just as children need to be calm in school to effectively learn, we all need calmness in order to grow, whether we are an employee or a manager, teacher or disciple, husband or wife, athlete or programmer. There is no activity or occupation that would not benefit from a measure of calmness.

Yet calmness is a perishable asset. It has an intangible quality, with no taste, shape, color, or smell of its own. We must tackle its cultivation creatively. It's no good to simply say "Calm down!" We need a concrete methodology to achieve ease in mind and body. In most respects, the mind controls the body, yet the condition of the body heavily influences quality of mind. Consider the experience of illness: when the body is under attack, the mind functions poorly. We are slow to respond, and often over-react as if surprised. We are irritable and unhappy. This suggests a critical concept: we can train the body to polish the quality of mind. We can learn to move with poise, precision and balance, and use our whole physique to accomplish tasks at hand. Through careful assessment of the efficiency of movement, we can analyze ourselves for excess tension, and use observation to study what our brain is doing.

This book features examples of the concrete, experiential mind-body coordination exercises employed at **AiShinkai** to center the body's physical balance, and to make that centering the focus of the mind's attention. Starting with simple movements - raising and lowering your arms, for example - these exercises are extremely effective tools for studying the mind's response to changes in posture. Human beings tend to lose concentration in changing circumstances. AiShinKai mind-body coordination exercises incorporate incremental challenges that foster tremendous resilience in the presence of change. This produces obvious improvement in our ability to apply the total assets of mind and body to any challenge.

One of the most important aspects of mind-body coordination training is the opportunity to work with a partner who can provide physical resistance to the movements. Carefully controlled challenges build confidence through the experience of success, and yields first-hand knowledge of the attributes of true self-mastery. The ultimate goal of AiShinKai training is to create new habits of physical experience so that the quality of mind can be honed to meet individual challenges and goals. For example, I use these exercises to cultivate the profound sense of calmness and resilience to change that helps me to be an effective educator, business leader, and martial arts competitor. It is a testment to the effectiveness of the system that these same exercises helped me to overcome a severe speech impediment, recover from serious injuries, and gain a reputation for composure and personal dignity in the face of the inevitable challenges that face every manager and board director. My daily regimen of martial arts training begins with these exercises. They bolster my greatest asset: a properly coordinated mind and body, and a sense of calmness and confidence that is the root - and natural product - of true self-mastery.

Addendum

The rich and diverse art of *Shodo* brush calligraphy provides a fun and playful means to experience and develop the calmness needed for success in daily life. Controlling the brush's delicate bristles in order to execute the proper shapes of Chinese and Japanese characters requires a profoundly relaxed mind and body. The artist must express an expansive spirit, and be attentive to the quality of line and the structure of composition. Excessive tension in the body yields unsteady strokes, just as the presence of mental agitation leads to poor control of stroke direction and placement. The immediate feedback provided by Shodo art writing, where each line can be brushed only in the moment and not corrected, provides a wonderful moment-to-moment snapshot of the conditions existing in body and mind.

This is one of the most wonderful aspects of engaging in the discipline and art of brush calligraphy: the artist can use the practice as a mirror to graphically reflect the qualitative condition of their experience. The results are immediate, tangible and obvious. Scholars, warriors, and civic leaders throughout history have admired Shodo as a means to polish character. It is a practical method to reveal the state of an individual's evolution towards the fullness of their humanity. This book provides an overview of Shodo's basic principles, tools, and practice. You are invited to play and experience for yourself the self-mastery that can be achieved through the art of Shodo brush calligraphy.

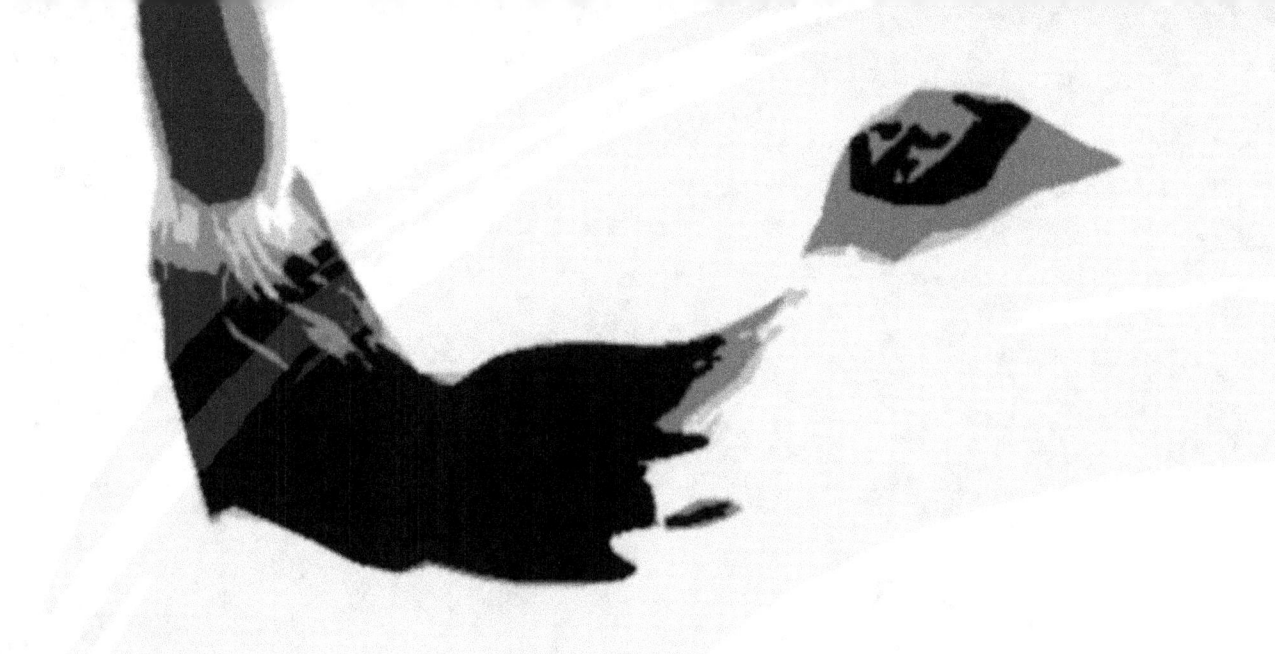

Part 1
From Simple Fun to True Self-Mastery

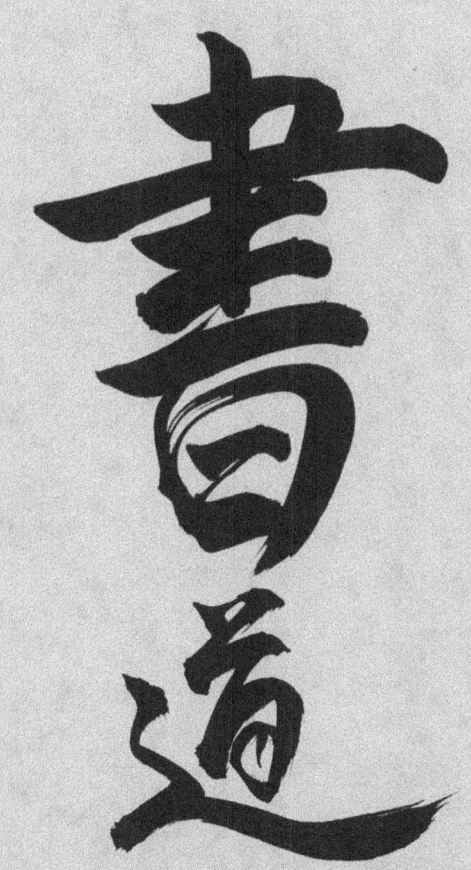

AiShinKai Publications
Self-Mastery in Daily Life
www.aishinkai.com

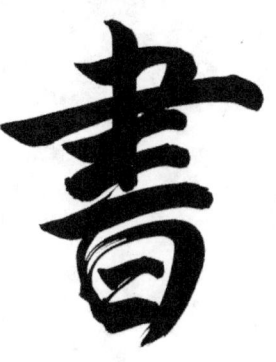

Shōdō Brush Calligraphy
From Simple Fun to True Self-Mastery

Dr. Jonathan Bannister, Ph.D./Ma.D.Sc.
AiShinKai Founder and President

Shodo, the "art of writing beautifully," is one of the most important traditional arts of Asia. Although originating in China, Japanese calligraphy is representative of that country's highly sophisticated culture of the late Heian period (1200's). It is studied and practiced by millions of people - from all ages and backgrounds - as a means to achieve self-development, artistic expression, and cultural awareness. Shodo encourages attentiveness to interactions, to our surroundings and the tasks at hand. Through diligent practice of the art, we can dramatically increase our ability to concentrate and our suppleness of thought. Both children and adults enjoy brush calligraphy. It is easy to get started, and only a little instruction in correct posture and technique brings quick rewards. Items needed to get started include the "four treasures:" a *fude* (筆) or brush, *washi* (和紙) calligraphy paper, a *suzuri* (硯) ink stone, and *sumi* (墨) ink.

In the spirit of the Confucian principle of *bun-bu-ryodo* (文武両道), "classical learning and martial arts are one," the samurai of old Japan studied brush writing for self-development, artistic expression, and cultural awareness. Shodo was so appreciated that at the time of the Meiji Restoration (1868), Japan's literacy rate was higher than that of Europe. For modern students, the art can be a tangible introduction to

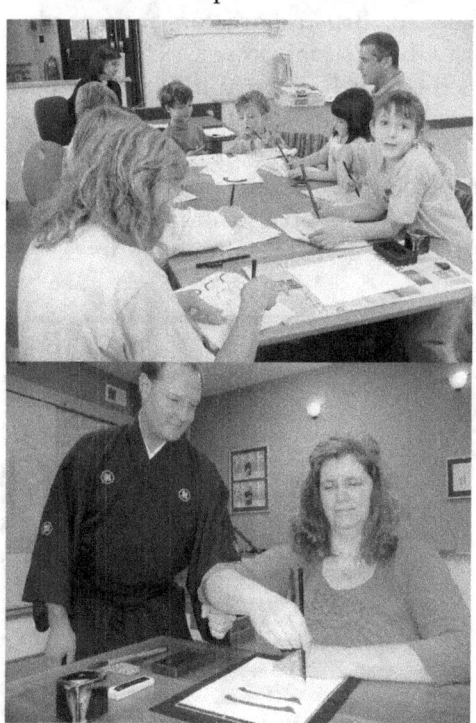

Asian culture and an important aid in the discovery of self-mastery. *AiShinKai* (Harmonious Heart Association) students practice brush calligraphy as an integral component of self-mastery training, holding equal place with a variety of other important martial and cultural arts such as *AiShin-Ryu Aikido*, *Iaido* Japanese swordsmanship, *Kyudo* traditional archery, *Ikebana* flower arranging, and *Bonsai*. AiShinKai's *Business Leadership*, *Conflict Resulution*, and *Team Management* programs employ techniques and exercises from Shodo brush calligraphy to illustrate and practice concepts of awareness and evaluation, visualization, and effective decision-making.

Brush calligraphy in the ancient Chinese styles presents multi-layered visual information in a manner that challenges artist and viewer to realize the potential of human beings to use integrated faculties. In the finest examples of the art, unity of the artist's body and mind gives rise to a spiritual power that enfuses even the barest of strokes with dynamic energy. The best brushwork magnifies the power of concepts hidden in the characters to hint at intuitive and elemental content. Most modern languages use phonetic symbols to represent the sounds used to construct words. With only a few symbols, one can create an endless vocabulary. In contrast, the Chinese and Japanese languages are based on pictographs and ideogrammatic characters. This poses a real problem during translation: characters represent conceptual, rather than literal ideas. Yet the system encourages tremendous subtlety in communication. Shodo artists draw out hidden meanings in characters to reveal inner content, and to present large ideas graphically. About two hundred elemental ideographs are the basis for an estimated 40,000-60,000 Chinese and Japanese characters.

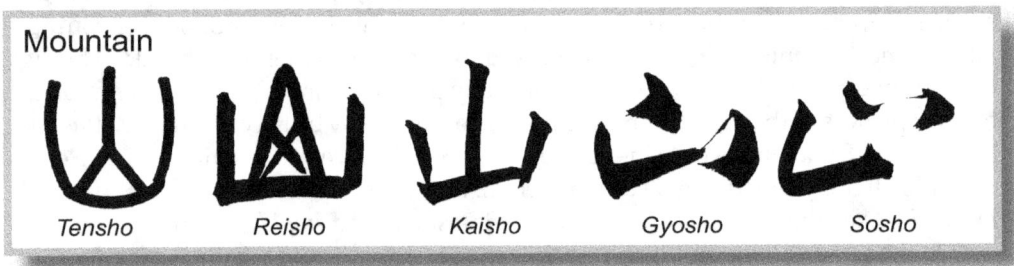

Mountain

Tensho   Reisho   Kaisho   Gyosho   Sosho

Development of Chinese and Japanese Characters

Kanji (漢字) Chinese characters originally evolved from markings made on bone and stone by priests interpreting the will of heaven. Brush characters are regarded as objects of reverence to this day, imbued with spiritual power. The Japanese borrowed the Chinese system of writing in the fourth century A.D., modifying the characters and structure to suit their own language. The Japanese still refer to the old scripts as "Chinese" characters, even though some of their shapes have undergone radical reinterpretation, and their names are pronounced very differently. The meanings of some characters have evolved differently in each country, making it difficult to translate some paintings, especially the oldest.

Five basic Chinese script styles were developed during different dynastic periods. *Tensho* (篆書), or seal script, is balanced and precise, and follows a set of rigorous rules established in China's Qin dynasty (221-206 B.C.). The forefather of all Chinese and Japanese characters, it is used primarily in ornamental seals printed on works of art and offical documents. The character of seal script is serious and dispassionate. Lines are drawn with even thickness, and the shapes of the characters generally fit into rectangles with a height-to-width ratio of either 3:2 or 2:3.

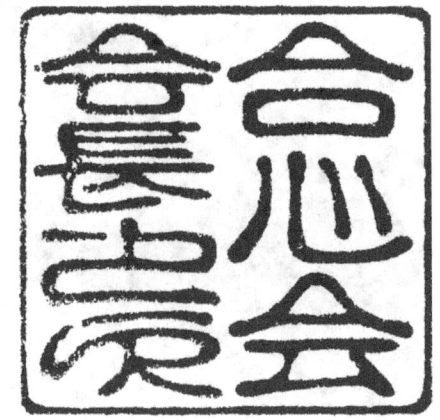

Reisho (隷書), or clerical script, developed in the Han dynasty (206 B.C. - 220 A.D.). It is a more user-friendly system suited to the everyday needs of scholars and administrative officials. Recognized by each character having a more or less horizontal, rectangular shape, its characters are drawn with a height-to-width ratio of approximately 2:3. Although the feeling expressed is serious and refined, many characters have at least one horizontal line that features a graceful flip to the right. This elegant touch softens the overall appearance.

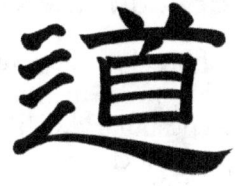

During the Han dynasty, a fluid and informal style called *Sosho* (草書), or "grass style" was also invented. Although a practical shorthand, with characters drawn with single, continuous brush strokes, the system gradually fell from favor: its extreme simplification and imprecision made it too difficult to read. However, its expressiveness and natural forms had a large impact upon the development of later styles. A less radical shorthand called *Gyosho* (行書), or "running script" was more successful. Developed in the Eastern Jin dynasty (317-420 A.D.) in southern China, this system is marked by fluidity, continuity of brush work, creativity of design, and relative ease of reading. This style is still much in use by artists in both China and Japan.

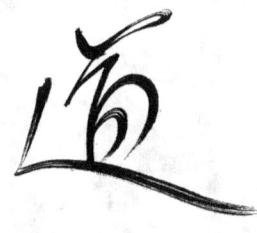

In the Tang dynasty (618-907 A.D.) a hybrid of seal and clerical scripts developed into a uniform, controlled, and elegant system called *Kaisho* (楷書), "correct" or block script. Following carefully prescribed rules that render characters easy to read, kaisho style writing has survived as the formal style of brush writing in the modern

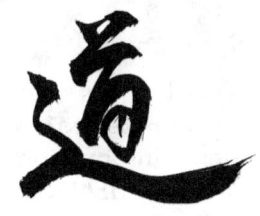

age. It is taught to students first because it ensures development of good technique. Kaisho features rhythmic brushwork caused by a movement pattern called *ton-dou-ton* (遯動遯), or stop-move-stop, that energizes and defines individual strokes. The style is recognized by an orderly structure and a sense of power.

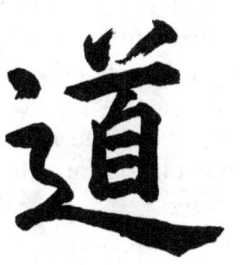

Modern Japanese calligraphers use all these styles, but kaisho, gyosho, and sosho styles predominate. In addition, the Japanese have created two alternative writing systems called *katakana* (片仮名) and *hiragana* (平仮名). The former are portions of Chinese characters read phonetically; they are rarely used in calligraphy. The latter are simplifications of Chinese characters, and are used with regularity, especially to express the sounds of words borrowed from other languages. Their simple, round shapes lend themselves to calligraphy, and they permit the Japanese to add grammatic devices like verbs and adjectives to the older Chinese characters.

Transcendental Writing

The art of Shodo is both an arduous discipline and an enjoyable recreation. The soft bristles of the brushes are difficult to control, but encourage a marvelously versatile vocabulary within the simplest of strokes. It is not enough to merely form the shapes of a character; lines, shapes, and volumes must be imbued with vigor and control. To achieve these qualities with a brush requires calmness, relaxation,

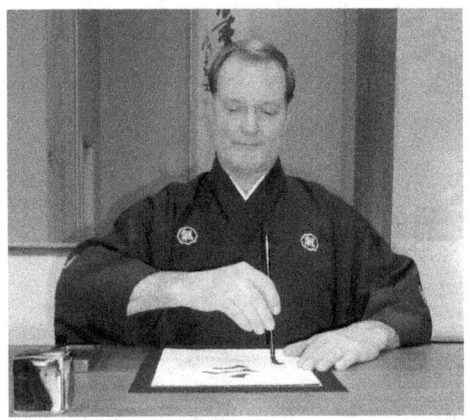

and concentration. This is where the greatest beauty of Shodo is revealed. To make art with a brush, the artist must look inward to examine the quality of his or her life experience. Agitation, discomfort, or distractedness are immediately revealed in the quality of brushwork and composition. Shodo is a highly polished mirror into which we can look to discover ourselves, as we are, *right now*. Through its discipline, we are encouraged to polish ourselves and work to become the person we most wish to be.

This book is intentionally only a beginner's guide to Shodo. You may ultimately wish to look at the resources listed at the end of the book for additional information. My goal is to introduce the core principles of Shodo as practiced at *AiShinKai*, and to briefly illustrate how this wonderful art can be used to cultivate self-mastery. Different sections will describe Shodo's basic principles, tools, and techniques, followed by worksheets with samples to copy, and illustrations to study and admire. To gain a better appreciation of the art, the advice of a qualified instructor is always invaluable, as is time spent reading books about asian art and culture, visiting museum and gallery collections, and attending shows of Shodo calligraphic art. To fully achieve the benefits of self-mastery - whether through the discipline of sword or brush - the most important elements are time, effort, and lots of practice.

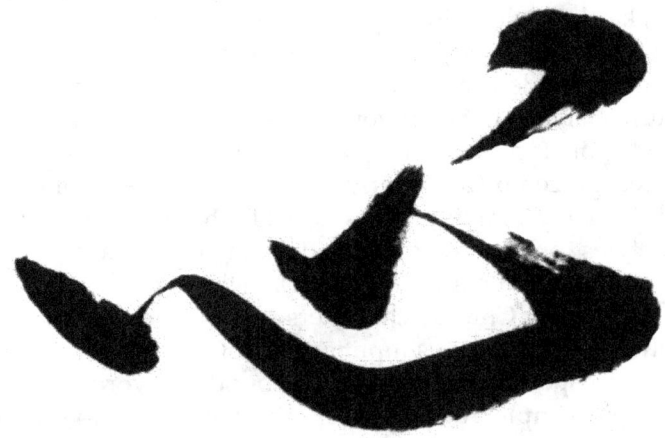

Kokoro (心) or *Shin* - "Heart" - the most important component of any endeavor.

16

The Tools of Brush Calligraphy

The Japanese understand that everything natural has a certain spirit. When a calligrapher needs to retire a brush, he will take it to a temple to thank it for its long 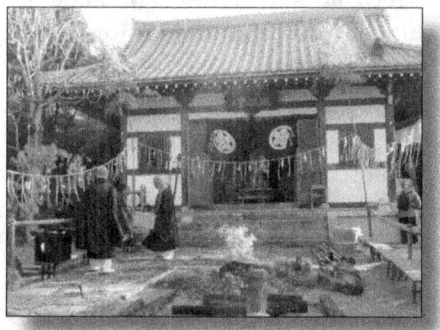 service. The brush is then ritually cremated in a ceremony called *Fude Kuyo* (筆供養). This is an indication of the respect and care that should be lavished on the tools of brush calligraphy. A single brush might cost hundreds of dollars, but even a ten-dollar *fude* (筆) will serve well for many years. When you are learning the basics, your brushes will be subject to a great deal of abuse, so handle them with kindness.

Only four pieces of equipment - the "Four Treasures of Shodo" - are essential to the practice of brush calligraphy:

> Ink stone (*suzuri*) 硯
> Ink (*sumi*) 墨
> Brush (*fude*) 筆
> Paper (*washi*) 和紙 or (*kami*) 紙

Five additional tools are helpful, but can be improvised:

> Calligraphy pad (*shitajiki*) 下敷 Any piece of felt larger than the paper will do.
> Water vessel (*suiteki*) 水滴 A bowl and spoon work well.
> Paperweight (*bunchin*) 文鎮 Anything clean, long and thin that distributes weight.
> Brush rest (*fudeoki*) 筆置 To keep the brush bristles from contacting the table.
> Sumi rest (*sumioki*) 墨置 The ink stick can be rested on a corner of the ink stone.

Proper care of these tools is extremely important. It is nearly impossible to draw beautiful characters with a damaged brush, or make good ink with a stone clogged with residue from old ink. Similarly, be attentive to the condition of your mind and the body, for these are your most important tools. Mind controls body, but the condition of your body will greatly influence your quality of mind. Breathing good air, getting enough sleep, and eating well are important to success.

Ink Stone: *Suzuri* (硯)

The *suzuri,* or ink-stone is made from a hard stone that has a fine, slightly abrasive texture against which an ink stick is gently ground and mixed with water to make *sumi* (墨) ink. This texture must be protected from scratches, and excess ink carefully washed off after each use. The stone is divided into two areas. The well is called *umi* (海), or ocean, and the grinding area is called *riku* (陸), or land. The ink stick should only be ground on the land, while the ocean holds clean water into which the ground ink is mixed. Natural stones are by far the best to use as the texture will make good ink. When chosing an ink-stone, go for a larger size. Since I travel a lot to teach, I use a stone measuring only 5" x 3" x 3/4", but this is a bit on the small

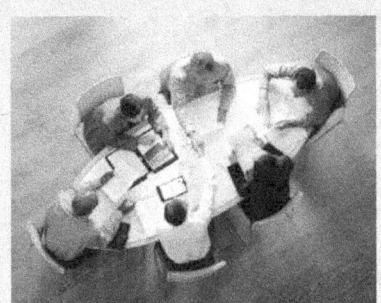

Brushing Your Way to
Leadership Skills

How Shodo Brush Calligraphy hones character, illuminates perception, and harnesses higher levels in the decision-making process

*C*arefully placing the tools, arranging the space, and settling oneself for a concentrated session of brush calligraphy is an exercise in cultivating self-mastery. There are so many lessons to learn in the process, and many parallels to the practice of leadership skills applicable in business, sports and daily life. Great leaders are motivated by personal values, and their vision of the future. They have an essential skill set common to all playing fields: concentration, calmness under fire, and the ability to perceive a big picture and enact a cogent program of coordinated action. Whatever innate talents an individual might start with, leadership ability must be developed through training, and it is absolutely in every organization's best interest to start effective succession planning and a leadership development program. All organizations need great leadership. The ability to manage should not be found only in top management; rather, everyone in the company should be encouraged to develop leadership skills. Leadership training should be part of every company's talent management strategy: it will pay ample dividends in lower recruitment costs, the ability to attract and keep top talent, increase employee productivity and satisfaction, and facilitate organization growth.[1] Key to the success of any program is scouting each candidate's natural talents, and helping them harness their natural capacity to focus, conceptualize, and act with clarity and decisiveness.

There are countless disciplines that encourage brain development, such as foreign languages and mathematics. Arts education is well-recognized for aiding the development of cognitive skills.[2] Exposure to fine and applied arts stimulates and developes imagination, critical thinking, and creativity. The arts cultivate craftsmanship, task performance quality assessment, and goal-setting abilities. Most importantly, the arts play a central role in cognitive, motor skill, language, and socio-emotive development.[3]

An encounter with *Shodo* brush calligraphy can be an important device for addressing the particular needs of developing leaders. **AiShinKai** Leadership Development, Conflict Resolution, and Team Management programs couple modern, win-win negotiation approaches with disciplines of mind-body coordination and classical arts education to foster unprecedented levels of self-mastery suitable to business, sports and daily life. We approach the goal of creating the next generation of social and civic leaders seriously, and encourage our students to use every discipline available to grapple with their developmental potential. Training in Shodo brush calligraphy is one of the powerful tools we use to illustrate and hone essential leadership principles and skills. The art requires a coordinated mind and body, which fosters the discovery of principles useful to achieve self-mastery. Shodo stimulates memory, enhances symbolic communicative skills, and provides an effective avenue for developing competence and confidence. Furthermore, the art provides an opportunity to encounter a different cultural perspective, and perceive alternative viewpoints and traditions. Calligraphy also provides a natural field of play, an integral tool to achieve learning and cognitive enhancement.[4] Finally, the discipline affords practitioners opportunities to introspectively consider Nature and to develop the profound calmness that is the root of moral judgement and effective decision-making.

[1] *Leadership Development Essentials*, 2010. http://www.leadershipdevelopmentessentials.com/businessleadershiptraining
[2] *Americans for the Arts*, 2002. http://www.artsusa.org/get_involved/advocacy/funding_resources/default_005.asp
[3] *Young Children and the Arts: Making Creative Connections*, 1998. http://www.artsusa.org/get_involved/advocacy/funding_resources/default_005.asp
[4] *My Work is My Play-The Journey from Survival to Creativity*, 2009. http://www.en8848.com.cn/Article/Others/Creativity/4640.html

To illustrate the graphic and leadership skill development power of Shodo, consider how leaders develop perception of problem scope and analyze applicable solutions. AiShinKai recognizes three stages of leadership development, as illustrated by the brush illustrations on this and the next page. Prior to the realization of leadership ability, a person's skills are applicable only to managing individual tasks. In the absence of a larger vision, beginning problem-solvers perceive only a disconnected series of isolated events or tasks. They have no ability to connect the dots, or even to understand the necessity of doing so. This individual may be counted upon only when tasks are clearly defined, and when coupled with regular assessment.

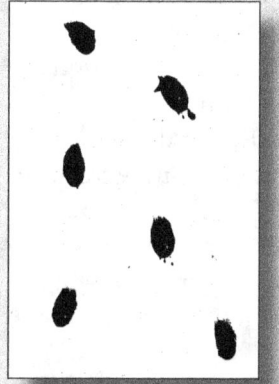

Level 1 Leaders understand that the organization has a mission, and that tasks at hand are related to one another. With the advent of initial leadership training, basic skills develop rapidly. They approach events with continuity, performing specific tasks with dependable precision developed by careful duplication of instructions received from a manager.

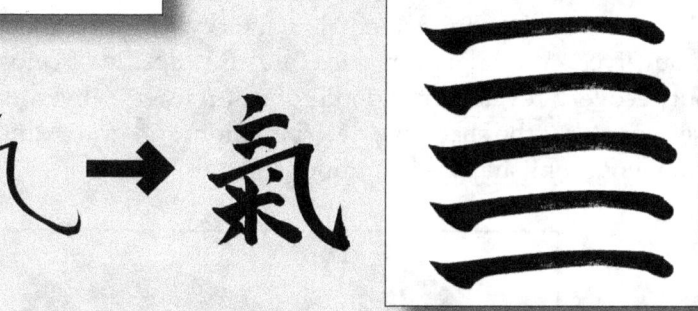

In the martial arts, this level of skill development is traditionally called *Shu* (守), a stage in which the student imitates the form and direction of the teacher. In Shodo, this level is marked by careful practice of *kaisho*, or block character forms. The student works to master the appearance and style of the characters, without a deep appreciation of the motivation driving their performance. Characters can be effectively produced, and can even be powerfully rendered, but the absence of any unifying vision prvents their performance rising to the level of art.

In this stage of development, the individual is building important tools for basic leadership. These include self-discipline and the ability to express ideas clearly and authoritatively. They can be counted upon to competently assist lower management with specific projects.

Level 2 Leaders have arrived at a stage in which they can reliably manage projects on their own. They clearly perceive the organization's mission from an *internal* point of view. In traditional martial arts this stage is called *Ha* (破), and is marked by mastery of form and the ability to subjugate the self to the task at hand. At this point, individuals exhibit flashes of real insight and creativity, and should be encouraged

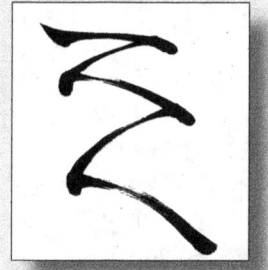

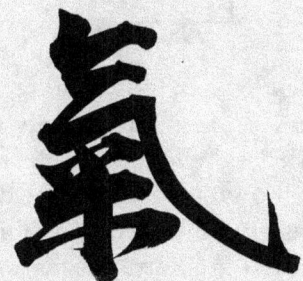

to seek out other points of view and experience. In Shodo, the artist is now capable of dependably demonstrating the results of great self-discipline and reliable technique. This corresponds to the *gyosho* style of semi-cursive calligraphy. Throughout this period of development, the student solidifies basic skills, takes ownership of the processes of command, and innovates new solutions. This is an exciting time for new leaders and for budding artists, yet it remains just one step on the longer path to true self-mastery.

Level 3 Leaders are the ultimate goal for an organization devoted to the cultivation of self-mastery and the development of future managers. Individuals at this stage discover a new freedom to depart from established forms. They have opened a door to truly creative technique, and arrived at a place in which action is directly and spontaneously taken in accordance with the intent of heart and mind. Though proceeding relatively unhindered, they are careful not to overstep the guiding principles and dictates of their art or field.

In martial arts, this stage of mastery is called *Ri* (離), and is thought to be unavailable except through the guidance of other masters. We believe that this experience is the natural birthright of all human beings, and AiShinKai orients its training programs towards that principle. Every person who dedicates themselves to the principles of self-mastery will ultimately be empowered to express leadership and innovative freedom within their chosen field of endeavor.

In Shodo, this experience of "breaking the mold" corresponds to *sosho* style calligraphy, true cursive writing. This is the style employed by great calligraphers through the ages to express innermost feeling in poetry and proverbs. To write beautifully in this manner requires complete mastery of form and technique, and with a resultant freedom of spirit stemming from that virtuosity.

Business, social, and civic leaders who have mastered the fundamentals of their craft become the "movers and shakers" who transform the fabric of our lives. While great masters are still capable of catostrophic failure, the style in which they bring about recovery reveals their depth of self-mastery. Even the great violinist Izhak Perlman occasionally misses notes, but the sheer joy, determination, and gracefulness with which he continues to play on in spite of momentary mishaps is inspirational.

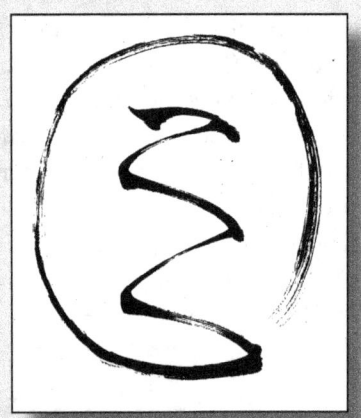

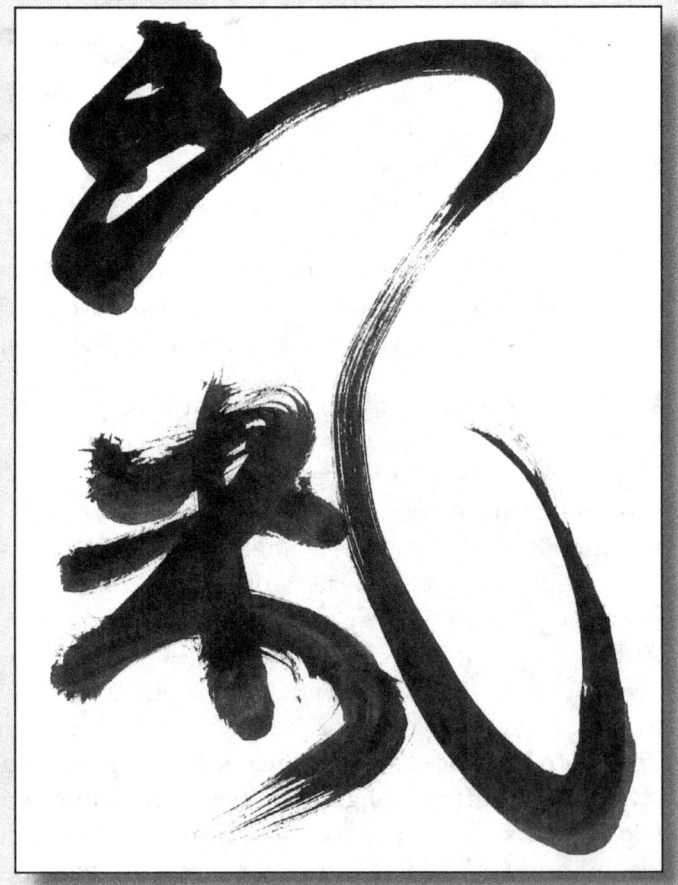

Great leaders perceive the unity of the whole. They possess the capacity to coordinate many tasks and events towards a higher purpose of their own invention. The difference between a master of Shodo brush calligraphy, a master of martial arts, or a master of business, social or civic strategy lies only in the medium of choice. For the student of leadership encountering Shodo as a means to achieve self-development, the strokes become analogous to the decision-making process and composition of solutions to be exercised in daily life.

size for comfortable painting. Decorated stones look nice, but you should choose a stone for its texture, not for how it looks on your desk. Buy a stone from a reputable store: not all are suitable for calligraphy. Avoid those made from ceramics or stone aggregates: the texture is wrong for making ink. Wash a new stone thoroughly with water and your fingers. Take care to avoid anything that might scratch the surface. The stone can be dried with a paper towel or soft cloth, or allowed to air dry.

To use the stone, first drip a bit of water into the stone's well. Now hold the ink stick vertically and extending out the bottom of your right fist. Wipe some water up unto the land, then begin drawing the end forward and backward in gentle, smooth strokes. *Some* pressure is required, but not a lot. My teacher used to say that the correct pressure was like that which could be exerted by a 10-year old. Periodically draw up more water to mix the ink, then push the mixture back down into the well. Be patient. Grinding ink takes five to ten minutes. Test your ink once in a while to see how it looks.

After painting, always remember to clean your stone (and brushes) before the ink dries. There is no faster way to ruin a stone than to allow ink to dry in it. You'll never be able to get it all off again. Wash your tools in clean water only, with no soap, using only your fingers. Be very careful not to scratch the stone. Pack away your tools in a safe, clean place when not in use: dirt, dust, and damaged tools are enemies to good calligraphy. Properly cared for, a good suzuri will last a lifetime or more.

Calligraphy Ink: *Sumi* (墨)

Your choice of ink is important. For quick practice sessions, prepared and bottled *bokujuu* (墨汁) liquid india ink may suffice, but for an aesthetically-pleasing, mind-calming, and spiritually-enriching experience, you should make a point of grinding your own ink from a sumi stick. Japanese calligraphy paper is thin, which allows the artist to control the application of ink to a high degree. This can be seen in the controlled appearance of blotting *nijimi* (滲み) and scratching *kasure* (掠れ) techniques used by calligraphy masters to add flair and visual interest to their artwork. The variations of ink application required to achieve these effects invariably causes the thin paper to buckle and warp. This is controlled by a process called *urauchi* (裏打), lightly re-wetting the paper and applying it to a supportive backing. The chemical bonds of your own ground ink will survive, but prepared ink bleeds and runs: your art will be destroyed.

It saves time and energy to use prepared inks; however, something intangible is lost in the process. Japanese brush calligraphy is a mental and spiritual exercise requiring concentration and application of one's whole human ability. Grinding your own ink provides an important opportunity to compose the mind and spirit, eliminate distractions, and focus on what you're going to try to communicate. You should feel free to use bottled, prepared ink to practice brush strokes and composition. But if you really want to create beautiful calligraphy, take the time to grind your own ink and experience real creativity.

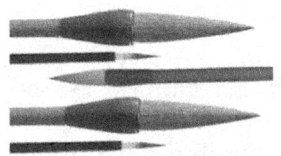

Brushes: *Fude* (筆)

There is much to learn about *fude* that is beyond the scope of this book. Beginner brushes should be 9-10 inches long with bristles that are 1.5"-1.75" long. Regardless of whether you buy an excellent brush or one of the least expensive, the process to prepare the bristles is the same. Brushes come with their tips starched in a way that restricts the forms that can be painted, so *gently* roll the bristles with your fingers to begin the process of separating them. Next, wash the brush in cold water to rinse out the starch. When the exposed bristles are pliable, you're ready to start painting. Shake out the excess water to reform the tip.

Every new brush takes time to master. Expensive brushes from reliable sources are manufactured to tight tolerances, so the time required to transition from old to new brush is considerably less. Inexpensive brushes require the same transition period, but only last a very short time, are prone to bristles falling out and damaging your calligraphy, and vary widely in feel, making it difficult to transition between them. Invest in a moderately good brush as soon as possible.

A couple of critical care tips: avoid scrubbing your calligraphy into the paper with a too-dry brush. This will damage both brush and paper. Always wash your brush before the ink dries. Brushes should be gently shaken to remove excess water and to reshape the tips before drying. Store brushes carefully to avoid damage. Some new brushes come with a protective plastic sleeve. You shouldn't store your brush in this sleeve as it will prevent drying. Replacing the sleeve can also seriously damage the bristles.

Paper: *Washi* (和紙) or *Kami* (紙)

Be forewarned: most inexpensive "calligraphy paper" is totally unsuitable for brush calligraphy. The problem is one of absorbancy: cheap papers soak up ink too fast. It is nearly impossible to avoid ugly *dango* (団子), or bulbous "dumpling" shapes forming at the ends of lines. This can be somewhat mitigated by thickening the ink, but there are practical limits. Cheap paper also tends to warp and buckle excessively. Good quality Japanese calligraphy paper is called *washi*. It is "sized" slightly on one side (the smooth side) with starch or clay to reduce absorbancy. This makes it ideal for controlling the flow of ink into the paper fibers. Some practice is required to achieve a balance between the thickness of the ink and the absorbancy of the particular paper being used. The difference in price between good paper and cheaper varieties is nominal, so invest and save your sanity.

All Japanese papers warp and buckle to some extent. To flatten the paper for mounting, paintings are misted to re-moisten them before gluing to a backing, a process called *urauchi* (裏打). This is why it is important to grind your own ink: prepared inks will bleed during the mounting process, ruining your artwork. Experiment with all kinds of paper until you find one that works for you.

Preparing Your Work Space

Prepare your work area by placing your tools in an arrangement that facilitates efficiency. This will help you concentrate, and to avoid spills and other mishaps. Note that all calligraphers paint with their right hands. It is extremely difficult to do Shodo with your left hand. The strokes must be painted left to right and top to bottom. Using the left hand results in a tragic mess as you cannot see what you're painting.

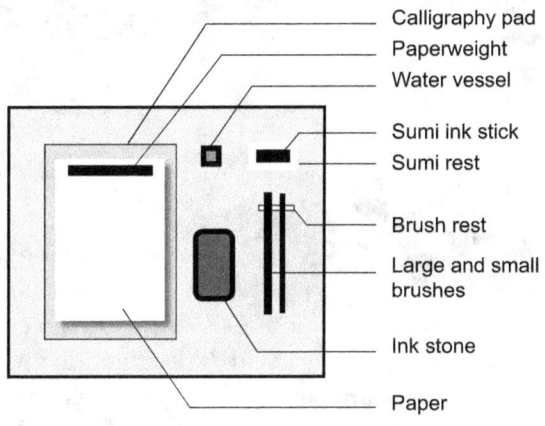

Calligraphy pad
Paperweight
Water vessel

Sumi ink stick
Sumi rest

Brush rest

Large and small brushes

Ink stone

Paper

Cultivating Your Strongest Natural State

Jazz singers create powerful statements by bringing into their music the depth of their life experience. In the same manner, your humanity will brings life and power to your calligraphy. To achieve peak performance in the discipline of Shodo requires a high degree of self-mastery and cultivation of a unified mind and body. Within the apparently simple act of brushing Chinese characters lie the seeds that reveal the astonishing range of human experience. Practicing brush calligraphy provides ample opportunity to do more than make a pretty drawing: you can seek to make your stongest natural state a truly dependable and transferable experience. What you discover through your brush will become applicable to all aspects of your daily life. Try to develop a feeling of calmness and relaxation. That way, your calligraphy can become infused with the kind of raw spiritual power seen in the finest works of Japanese and Chinese masters. Make even the most spare of your strokes an affirmation of a decision to "live a life worth living."

The *AiShinKai* **Basic Principles of Shodo: Brush Calligraphy** interpret and expand core principles of **AiShinKai** self-mastery training to specifically help artists achieve mind-body coordination, brush control, and visual sensitivity.

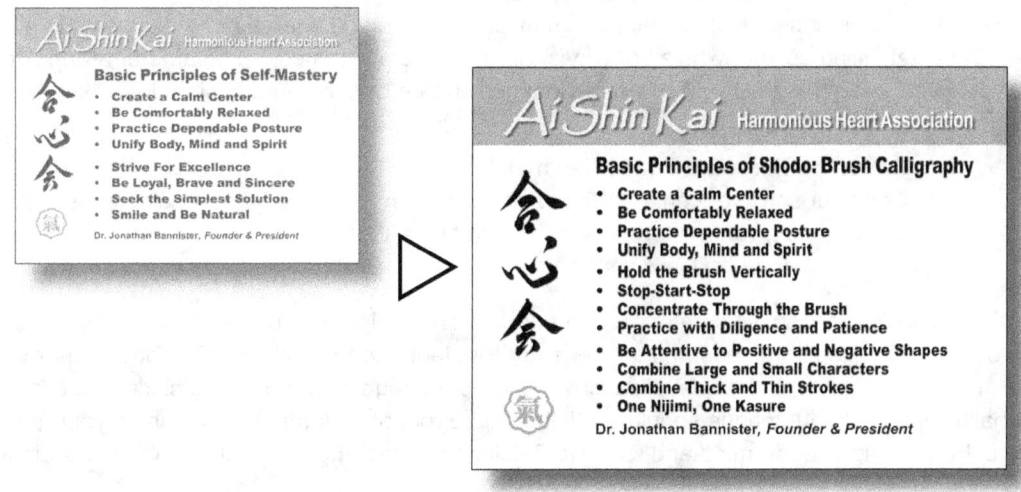

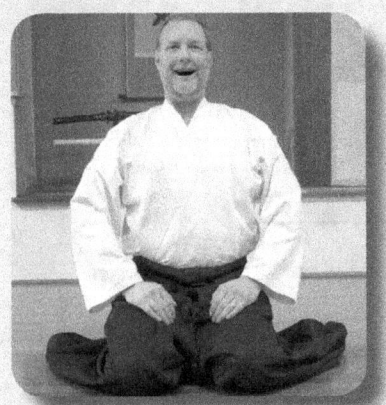

AiShinKai Breathing and Meditation Exercises

Reprinted from *The Path to Self-Mastery: Lessons from the Martial Arts to Achieve Peak Performance in Business, Sports, and Daily Life* (**AiShinKai** Publications 2011)

It's weird, but it works! Many activities use breathing and meditation exercises to cultivate calmness, relaxation, and focus. The development of these exercises in the martial arts is lost in the mists of time, yet their forms remain especially relevant to to the challenge of meeting high performance demands since in practice they include a high degree of wakefulness. Many of us lead relatively inactive lives, with little attention given to the correct coordination of mind and body. The demands of high performance in any field generates stress, which in turn results in poor health and mind-body disunity. Breathing and meditation exercises promote attentiveness, calmness, relaxation, and good health. They facilitate oxygen exchange, and allow careful observation of natural technique and physical rhythms. This fosters self-confidence and the development of a positive attitude. AiShinKai's meditation exercises are specifically designed to help focus the mind on the body's center of balance. Attention and awareness are then extended outwards from this clearly identified center, and a platform is created from which it becomes possible to spring forward on the path to higher performance, balance, and effectiveness in all activities of daily life.

Breathing Technique (perform early in the morning when the surrounding air is freshest)
Sit comfortably on your knees, or on the front edge of a chair. It's important to have your feet properly aligned with your knees and hips. Breathe in through your nose, settling your breath into the center of the lower abdomen. Support the breath, but do not hold it. Using your diaphram for control, open your mouth wide as if to say "AH" and allow both the air and your mind to extend outwards over the horizon. Avoid excess tension in the throat or mouth. Bow forward slightly to naturally compress the remaining breathe from your lungs, then close your mouth and gently inhale. Rise again to expand the chest cavity. Repeat this process for 5-10 minutes. As you become more relaxed the cycle will elongate: 45-60 second cycles are an ultimate goal, but seek to find a comfortably sustainable rhythm for yourself.

Meditation Exercises (immediately following the Breathing Technique)

1.   **Meditation on an infinitely small Center** (2-5 minutes)
     Maintain your center, envisioning a basketball-sized sphere centered in the lower abdomen. With every exhalation, the sphere shrinks in diameter by half, eventually reaching a sense of the infinitely small.

2.   **Meditation on infinite extension** (2-5 minutes)
     Maintain your sense of an infinitely small center. Imagine energy or light gushing in all directions from your center, filling up your whole body. Visualize a sphere two meters in diameter around you, centered in the lower abdomen. With every exhalation, this sphere of energy extension doubles in size, leading to a sense of the infinitely large.

3.   **Meditation on Personal Space** (2-5 minutes)
     Maintain your sense of center. With each exhalation, your energy extension sphere decreases in size by half and gradually returns to yourself. Eventually establish a sphere two meters in diameter, centered in your lower abdomen. This is your personal space, the area your body can reach with an arm or leg.

During each exercise, sit comfortably and upright on the floor or front of a chair. Three points of contact with the floor are ideal for stability: knees and tail bone, or both feet and tail bone. Softly focus your eyes about two meters in front of you. Many people find visualizations easier to manage with their eyes closed, but this can cause sleepiness and hallucinations. Your tongue should lightly touch the roof of your mouth just behind your teeth to reduce the flow of saliva. Feeling big in body, mind and spirit will facilitate relaxed engagement with your surroundings. (題)

Basic Principles of Shodo

#1 Create a Calm Center

In addition to communicating character content, great calligraphy reveals the artist's mental state and degree of self-mastery. Calmness is essential in every discipline, but it's not enough to merely command ourselves (or anyone else, for that matter!) to "calm down." We need a positive tool to achieve this goal. To stabilize mind and body, try to focus on a point at the center of your body's mass.

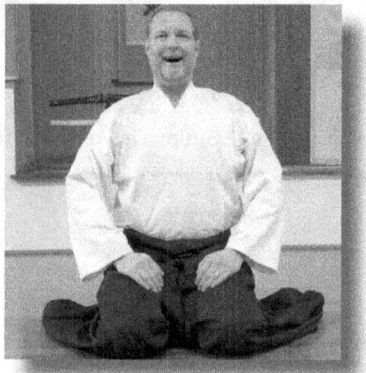

While standing or sitting, this point is located in the lower abdomen, at the level of the pelvic bone but deeper inside. It is a location that can't be consciously tightened by muscle. If you make this point the focus of your attention, you will be better able to maintain a center of balance. Your mind will naturally reside at the center of your body, and great calmness will result. Practice makes this experience habitual and dependable. Cultivating a dependable natural state is a pre-condition to effective painting, so give it a try!

AiShinkai **Breathing and Meditation Exercises** are very helpful tools that create a calm sense of center. If you are not calm, your attempts to control the brush will be exhausting, if not actually frustrating. It requires sensitivity to feel the interaction of brush and paper. Moreover, tremendous concentration is needed to compose positive and negative shapes in relation to one another. But even the greatest effort, if not applied in the right way, will only produce an agony of disjointed, inelegant strokes, disconnected to the whole. Sometimes the hand that holds the brush shakes uncontrollably. This is usually caused by mental agitation and excess tension in the body. Taking time to compose yourself and to coordinate your mind and body will help you to produce far better results. It's never the fault of brush, ink, or paper if a character cannot be produced as envisioned. When mind and body are properly composed, the brush accurately expresses internal states as well as intent, and ink flows across the paper as naturally as over a waterfall.

Basic Principle #2: Be Comfortably Relaxed

Correct physical posture (*shizen-tai* 自然体) is important to establishing brush control. Consider the stress caused by excess mental tension. It is harmful to health, causes poor judgment, and leads to physical tension and loss of fine motor control. Mind controls body, but the condition of the body influences the quality of mind. Our bodies have two sets of voluntary muscles: extendors and contractors. When we are tense, each set engages and cancels out the efforts of the other. Net power approaches zero, and physical movements can't be performed efficiently. In Shodo, for example, the delicate control required to handle the brush is elusive in the presence of mental or physical stress. AiShinKai training is designed to encourage relaxation without the sacrifice of correct form. Our Mind-Body Coordination Exercises can be used to analyze the quality of physical movement and reveal the condition of Mind. Training partners help by providing gentle resistance and balance checks to give feedback. Stiff arms produce stiff characters, so take time to calm down before attempting Shodo.

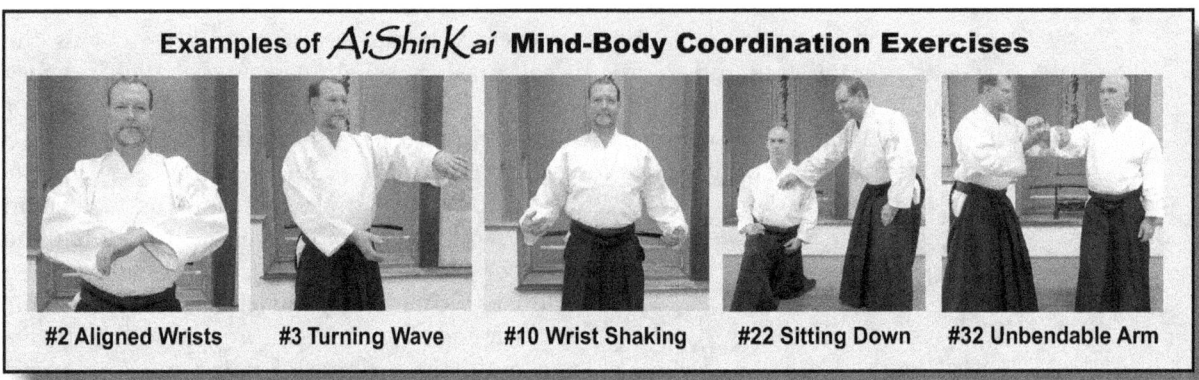

Examples of *AiShinKai* **Mind-Body Coordination Exercises**

#2 Aligned Wrists #3 Turning Wave #10 Wrist Shaking #22 Sitting Down #32 Unbendable Arm

Basic Principle #3: Practice Dependable Posture

Traditionally, Japanese and Chinese calligraphers painted at a low table while sitting on the floor. This is uncomfortable for modern practitioners of Shodo. A work table and a straight-backed firm chair are good choices. Sit erect on the front of the chair, and position yourself about one fist's distance from the edge of the table. Your left hand will support the bottom of the paper, while a paperweight holds the top. Your left elbow should be positioned about one fist from the edge of the table. Tuck in your tail bone, straighten your spine, and *gently* engage the muscles of your abdomen and groin. Lean forward slightly towards your work space. In the beginning, it may be helpful to have someone test the dependability of your posture before you paint. You'll only need to do this a few times to experience correct posture. Tests should be gentle and conducted in a spirit of cooperation. They should help you to calm down, relax, and center. It is *not* a competition!

Helpful tests include 1.) checking the stability of your torso by gently pressing the front of a shoulder towards your center; 2.) gently lifting your right elbow as you practice basic strokes. If your posture is correct, your arm will be naturally heavy and immovable. Mind and body will be correctly coordinated and internal energy can be expressed through your brush.

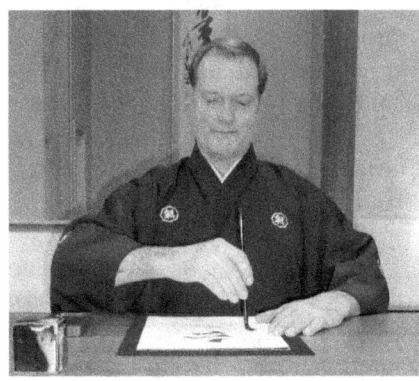

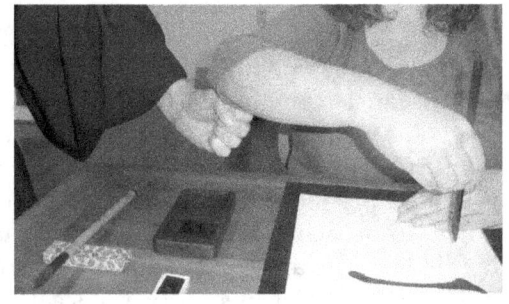

Testing dependable posture helps the calligrapher develop self-mastery.

26

Basic Principle #4: Unify Body, Mind & Spirit

We know that mind controls body, and that the condition of the body influences the quality of mind. To a large degree, our intentions determine our actions. When sick or seriously injured, we feel sluggish or unable to concentrate. This link between mind and body is very strong. When working effectively together, mind and body wield power hugely in excess of the sum of their parts. For lack of a better word, we call that "spirit." We could also say fortitude, or courage, will-power, guts, or life force. We might borrow from Japanese and use the word "*Ki* (氣)," or the Chinese "*Chi,*" or the Hindi word "*prana.*" For the sake of simplicity we use the word "spirit" - not in any religious sense - but as "full of spirit" or "spirited." When we combine strong will with mind-body coordination, we become nearly unstoppable. AiShinKai training develops this coordination into a conscious and dependable lifestyle, an experience made habitual through the achievement of incremental success.

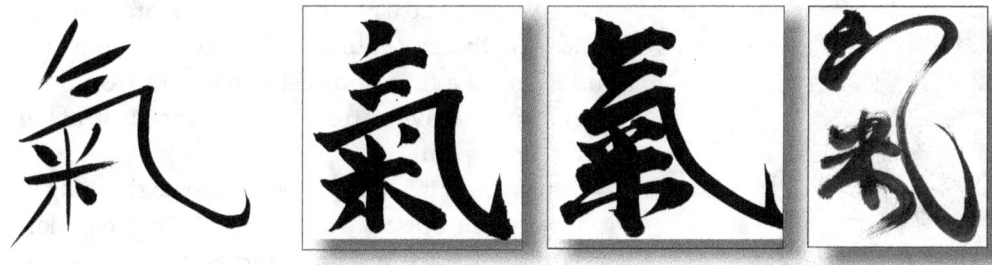

Four renditions of "*Ki* (氣)," or spiritual energy: a pictogram representing rice cooking over fire that suggests internal, simmering power. The left sample, while legible, exhibits weak brushwork, while the three examples to the right - featuring *kaisho*, *gyosho*, and *sosho* styles - are powerful, focused, and radiant with energy. In each case the character's content is illuminated; the brush strokes are firm and exhibit control of form and expression.

Full-spirited experience lends intensity to the brushstrokes of Shodo, while its absence results in strokes lacking sincerity. Don't confuse this with mere weight of stroke: *sosho* style writing can be ethereal, even wispy, like smoke. Rather, when the artist commands his or her full human potential, Shodo writing becomes enormously expressive and commanding. We will discuss the form of well-defined, *Ki*-filled strokes in Part 2: Practice Samples.

Basic Principle #5: Hold the Brush Vertically

The correct way to hold the brush is sometimes called "lady's hand." Hold the brush in the middle of the handle, with relaxed fingers naturally extending towards the bristle end. This is sensible, as this is where your mind must be focused (see Principle 7). Rest the brush between your index and middle fingers, and secure its position with your thumb. The fourth (ring) and little fingers do not touch the brush, but should be in contact with each other, and touching the middle finger. Kerep your hand relaxed and slightly cupped. Due to nature of Shodo brush strokes, your arm and the brush must be free to move in any direction. To achieve this, hold the brush vertically. The tip should be angled slightly to the right, and

27

Brush, Sword, and Pen are One

Dr. Jonathan Bannister, Ph.D./Ma.D.Sc.

AiShinKai Founder & President

In 1987 my Aikido teacher allowed me to observe him brushing formal certificates for rank promotion. I was impressed by his careful preparations, intense concentration, and utter commitment to perfection. It was clear that he considered his task very seriously. His calligraphy was precise; the strokes sure. The results were beautiful. Watching my teacher's attitude, posture and breathing, I clearly saw a connection between martial arts and calligraphy.

Regardless of whether I take a brush, or a sword, or a pen in hand today, the foundation skills I have developed over thirty years in the martial arts inform my abilities. Many masters before me have observed that Shodo, Japanese swordsmanship, and great leadership have much in common. All require calmness,

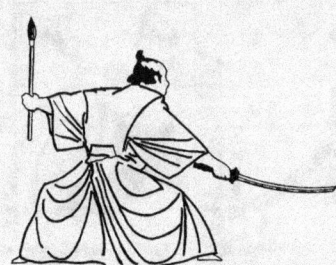

attentiveness, and a resolute spirit. Before entering a martial arts contest, I make sure that my equipment is in good order. I take time to calm myself, and identify a firm and resilient center from which to act. Entering the arena, I check my posture, and meet the task at hand with a unified body, mind, and spirit.

In swordsmanship, every action begins long before the actual weapon is drawn. The opponent, whether real or imaginary, must first be engaged with the mind. Eura Kazunori Sensei, a great swordsmanship teacher in Tokyo, Japan, describes the need to "suppress the opponents *Ki*," his spiritual power. Once a decision to draw is made, the sword's movement is driven forward from the center of your body. Consider the horizontal draw called *nukitsuke* (抜付): the touch to the handle must be so light that the blade can be twitched forward by the grip, rather than by the force of the arm. The sword is pressed forward to forestall the capacity of the oponent to resist. Upon contacting the target, the grip is firmed; only then is the unified power of body and mind applied. Nothing can be left behind. The cut must be focused to the target, and the motion of the sword arrested before an opening is created into which the opponent could counter-attack. Throughout the action, calmness must be maintained, or the swordsman risks losing control of the weapon, or even worse: he may lose his humanity to ego.

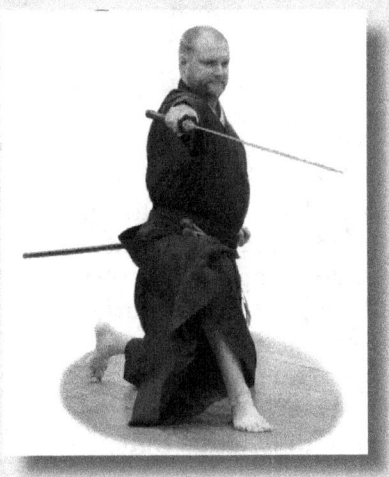

My experience of brush calligraphy is remarkably similar: tools must be ordered and maintained, quality of mind honed, posture and  spirit harnessed, and contact with the paper occurs long before the actual stroke is made. To touch the paper is to reach a target, and the *ton-dou-ton* rhythm of the brush expresses natural decisiveness. Control is maintained according to the requirements of the characters' form and the composition desired. Finally, a special quality critical to Japanese martial and cultural arts called *zanshin* (残心), continuous mind, allows the artist to move mind and brush freely from character to character. There is no

difference between the experience of drawing a sword and delivering a decisive cut, and the punctuation of brush strokes in Shodo.

In many sword forms a final overhead, downward cut concludes the combative phase of a technique. This cut must be made with great resolve, and exhibit what swordsmen refer to as *Ki-Ken-Tai-Ichi* (気剣体一), Spirit-Sword-Body-Oneness. The cut must be straight, accurate, focused at a specific target, and be well-connected to one's center. Vertical strokes in Shodo should possess the same content. In order to express a strong spirit, vertical lines should be firmly anchored to a point at the top of the stroke, then pulled resolutely towards one's center. Once again, the content of the calligraphic stroke is remarkably similar to that in swordsmanship. The same content is found in the martial art of Aikido, a Japanese throwing/grappling system. Once attackers are redirected out of their stable posture, their balance can be taken with a downward, sweeping lead. Little force is required, yet the results are spectacular. A similar coordinated spirit and composure form the platform needed in Kyudo, Japanese traditional archery. Without a correct physical posture and fullness of spirit, the bow cannot be controlled and arrows fly errantly.

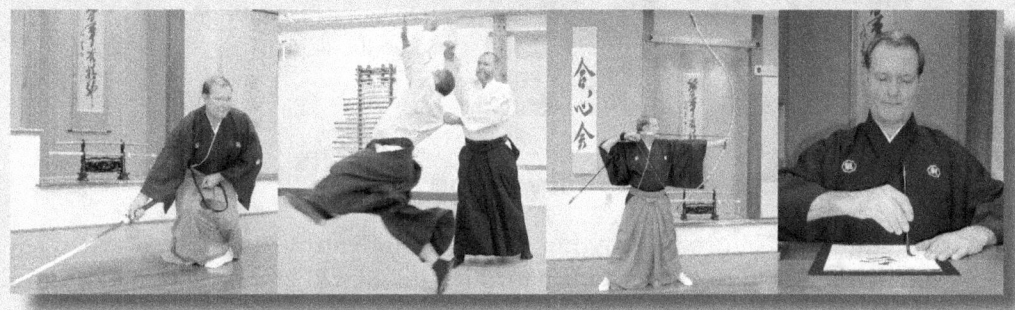

The unified power of mind and body is a key tool for those who would exercise leadership, or experience success in martial arts or brush calligraphy. So closely aligned is the spirit in which these arts should be practiced that AiShinKai classes of all kinds use Shodo calligraphic illustrations to communicate delicate points of practice. Everyone learns differently, and an individual may not always grasp the content of a verbal or physical explanation. A graphic representation of a difficult concept or technique can be instructive and helpful.

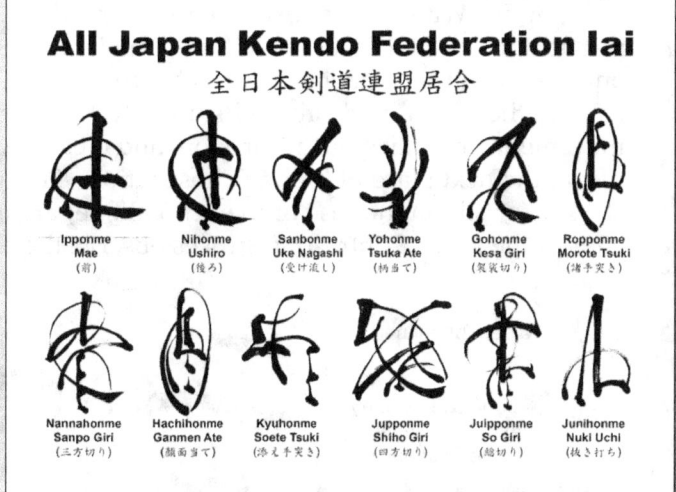

Calligraphic representations of All Japan Kendo Federation basic sword techniques.

Great calligraphy, inspired leadership, and superior martial arts all require great heart. It is not necessary to envision doing battle while practicing calligraphy, but it is desirable to brush with sincerity. Shodo is much more than writing characters; it is a means to beautifully and powerfully express the inner content of ideas, and to reveal the fullness of our development as human beings. 氣

directed slightly towards your center. Your right hand shouldn't touch the paper: instead, the arm is suspended to allow complete freedom of movement. Don't try to move the brush with just your wrist. Your whole arm should motivate the brush from your center (Principle 1). To ensure smooth movement, horizontally suspend your right elbow with a slight *floating* feeling that is positively connected to your center through the natural heaviness of relaxation (Principle 2). This will encourage dependable posture (Principle 3). Try feeling as if you are resting your right elbow on an imaginary sphere of light or energy arising from your center. That will help you to brush with unified mind and body (Principle 4).

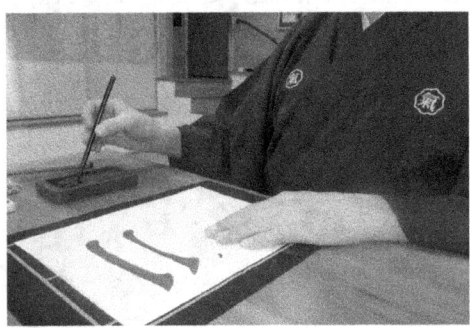

Dip the brush into the well (*umi* 海 "ocean") of the ink stone. Take care to preserve the pointed tip of the brush as you wipe away excess ink on the grinding area (*riku* 陸 "land"). The brush should be saturated without being inclined to drip. If dripping is a problem, consider grinding more ink to thicken the liquid.

Basic Principle #6: Stop-Move-Stop (遜動遜)

Everything in Nature has rhythm. We exist in Nature, and to achieve efficiency we should strive to move with natural timing. Otherwise, our actions will be unnatural, and the results unstable. In Shodo, this principle is called "*ton-dou-ton* (遜動遜)," or stop-move-stop. This essential rhythm defines the strokes of brush calligraphy. Without it, strokes are weak and the eye is provided with no place to rest as it follows the strokes. At "stop" points, visualize the character and pause only momentarily to allow ink to absorb into the paper. Next, slightly lift the base of the brush, and proceed smoothly to the next "stop" position. Smooth movements minimize ink absorption, and create dynamicism. Brush and eye will rest at the next place of high ink absorption. Study the examples below: the top strokes (or left, in the case of the vertical line) are made without definition at the ends of the lines. Contrasting strokes observe the principle of stop-move-stop.

Weak, undefined

Strong, with clearly defined beginning, middle, and end

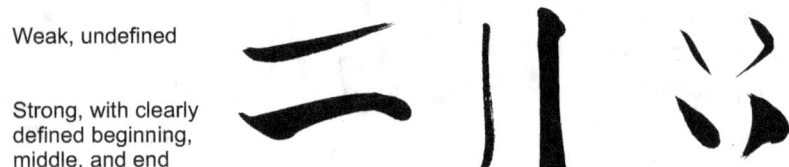

This principle suggests an essential corollary of observing proper stroke order. Kanji characters should be written in a manner that resembles water cascading down a mountainside, with strokes descending in clear, vertical sequence just as gravity would dictate. Observing the stop-move-stop principle makes the logical sequence fairly obvious. The practice samples in Part 2 are numbered to indicate stroke order.

Basic Principle #7: Concentrate Through the Brush

Be a child who loves to paint. Gradually exert some control in your play by becoming more aware of your posture and breathing. The brush is an extension of your body and mind, just like the finger that you use to point. You don't have to think about how to point and touch: your mind extends through the finger naturally and spontaneously. Next, become aware of the contact that the brush has with the paper: too much pressure will break the bristles, too little produces only thin lines. Experience the *inochi-ge* (命毛) - the bristles at the center of the brush - gently scratching the paper. Enjoy the rhythm made as they release tension and friction. Now experiment with gently fanning the bristles to release more ink, and changing speeds in multiple strokes and directions. Listen for the sensual and captivating sounds the brush makes on the paper. Playing in this way will help you to build a rich, personal vocabulary of thick and thin strokes, punctuation and fluid lines. Once you understand the brush's capabilities, you can consider how to draw characters that express your idea of their meaning.

Basic Principle #8: Practice with Diligence and Patience

The details of any discipline can seem confusing at first. Through practice, we train to make basic movements automatic. But each character, and every change in paper or brush, brings new and fresh challenges. No moment is ever exactly the same. We teach our students to face this challenge by calming the mind, focusing on their center of balance, and by embrace their surroundings with mind-body coordination. This requires considerable practice: the mind can only do one thing at a time, and there is a great temptation to focus on one condition of practice at the expense of all others.

Learning is a natural process that we should learn to approach deliberately and carefully. In doing so, we can train the mind to embrace many aspects of a technique from multiple planes of experience. A beginning archer is overly-conscious of the relationship between himself and the bow. Once basic forms are mastered, the target draws attention. Only in later stages of development does the archer experience the Self, and the bow, arrow, and target as merely different aspects of one technique, even one thought. The same is true in Shodo. In the beginning, we are our own worst enemy. We struggle for control, but there is too much to master. Posture and breathing, brush, ink, characters, . . . each resists every attempt to impose order. Concentrating on one aspect throws that element out of proportion to the rest of the painting.

It is best to suspend judgement. In the beginning, your best efforts will not be masterful. Accept this, and engage in the process required to gain skill whle-heartedly. Self-criticism (as opposed to analysis) and frustration do nothing to inspire improvement. Shodo is a particular path that can lead to extraordinary awareness, sensitivity, and depth of understanding through the achievement of self-mastery. It is a fascinating discipline that requires time and practice.

Basic Principle #9: Be Attentive to Positive and Negative Shapes

Mastering how to position the positive and negative shapes of characters in relation to their centers of balance will determine most of your initial success with drawing calligraphy characters. From the moment we graduate from crawling to walking, we begin to take balance for granted. Of course, visual and mental balance is created and sustained only through active practice. The appropriate position and relative size of characters in a composition is subject to an analysis of their meaning, while the overall axis of visual balance is determined by their shapes.

The axis of visual balance becomes especially important when arranging multiple characters in a composition. Layouts that misplace centerlines create competing shapes in positive and negative space. Each character must be drawn to carefully control the tensions created or risk displeasing the eye.

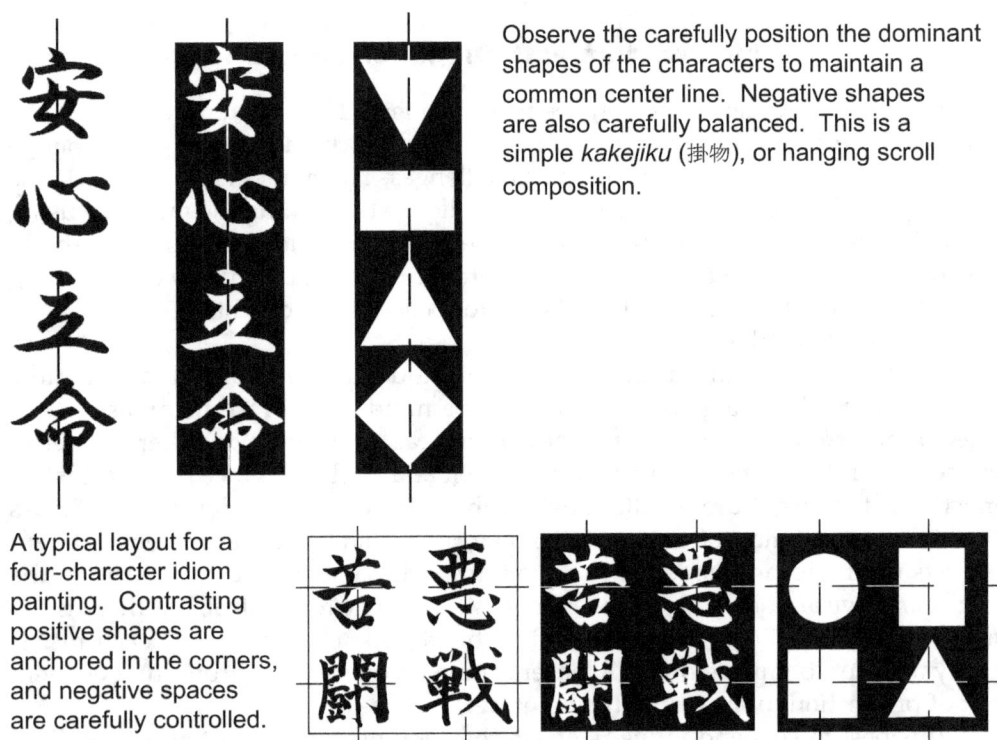

Observe the carefully position the dominant shapes of the characters to maintain a common center line. Negative shapes are also carefully balanced. This is a simple *kakejiku* (掛物), or hanging scroll composition.

A typical layout for a four-character idiom painting. Contrasting positive shapes are anchored in the corners, and negative spaces are carefully controlled.

Basic Principle #10: Combine Large and Small Characters

A white subject on a white background becomes invisible, and a composition with characters all the same size is less effective in propelling visual interest and understanding. It is through contrast that we perceive meaning. A particular character might be emphasized, with others relegated to supportive roles. There are masterful examples that demonstrate effective contrast included at the end of this book. Some *kakejiku* (掛物) hanging scrolls show changes in character size within the midst of *sosho*, full-cursive, single lines of multiple *kanji*. These are truly the effort of masters: it is wonderfully difficult to vary character shape and size in mid-flow and still manage to maintain the effectiveness of the composition.

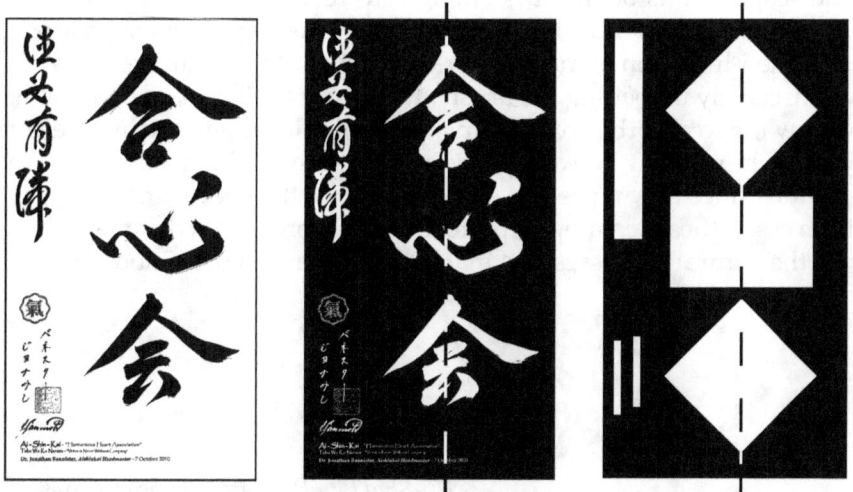

A more complex layout with variation in character size and an assymmetrical balance.

Basic Principle #11: Combine Thick and Thin Strokes

Using a variety of stroke weights also contributes to visual interest and the dynamicism of a composition. Line weights can be increased by increasing pressure to the brush, which causes the bristles to fan out and release more ink.

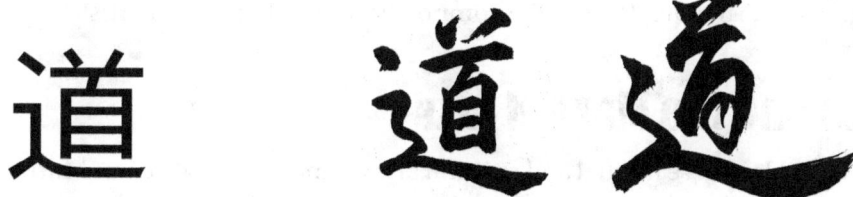

Compared to the typeface character on the left, the Shodo examples to the right are more dynamic and humanistically-expressive. This impression is created by subtle variations in stroke thickness and shape. These attributes become most pronounced in *gyosho* style writing, as shown on the right.

Basic Principle #12: One *Nijimi*, One *Kasure*

The formal practice of Japanese Shodo brush calligraphy has many well-defined rules governing the art. They may not be suitable for consideration by every beginner, but consider incorporating some of these principles as you improve. The presence and positioning of *nijimi* (滲み), or blotted areas, and *kasure* (掠れ), scratchy areas, are considered critical to the success and artistic balance of higher works of Shodo art. The placement of these elements, together with the beauty of the script, defines the artistic value of the work. There should be at least one of each in every piece. There are many such rule - for example, two blotted or scratchy characters should not appear adjacently - but such considerations are well beyond the scope of this book. It is enough fto recognize and appreciate them, and consider adding their attributes to your repertoire as you make progress. Be assured that their inclusion in master works is deliberate. Nijimi are blots created either by consciously unloading the brush after it is first dipped, or by pausing the brush to allow ink to absorb profusely in a particular location. Kasure are created either by rapid movement, or with a dry brush. They each add dynamic appeal to compositions since they represent extreme ends of the spectrum of calligraphic line. In both cases, these seeming imperfections are considered desireable because they reveal the natural processes and materials that are used in Shodo.

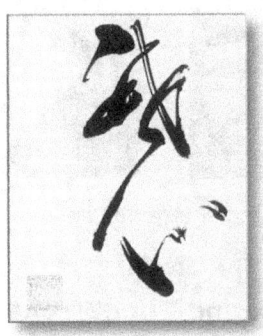

Bu-Shin (武心) "Warrior Mind" by master calligrapher Masaaki Hatsumi. His fine *sosho* brushwork incorporates both *nijimi* and *kasure* in a lovely composition evoking the ethereal nature of a soldier's life.

You can see many examples of excellent and masterful calligraphy in Part 3. It is worth the effort to read books about asian art, visit galleries with calligraphy displays, and attend calligraphy shows. It takes some effort to train your eyes; the balance and dignity of fine calligraphic art can be elusive. Seek out applications of Principles 9-12 in the compositions of other Shodo artists.

Shodo and the Martial Arts

I have studied Japanese martial and cultural arts for more than 30 years. Maruyama Shuji Sensei, my Aikido teacher, first introduced me to *Shodo* brush calligraphy. As I practiced, it became obvious that the rigors and principles of the martial arts were also present in the discipline of Shodo.

It happened at a national training seminar for Aikido, many years ago. I had been training in martial arts for more than ten years, and had been teaching for 3 years. Despite my experience, I was about to experience a complete loss of composure and a serious challenge to my spiritual fortitude. I was partnered with a particularly senior teacher in regular weapons class. Though not a large man, it was clear that he possessed a dominant will. We briefly exchanged of series of strikes to test each other's metal. Then the instructor known as "The Tiger" proceeded to share with me a special lesson about what it meant to be a martial artist, and what it meant to be fully human. Without warning, he launched a full-bore, continuous attack, raining blows and bearing down on me with a ferocity I had never before encountered. There was no time to think, and no place to escape. No technique, trickery, or strategy that I knew made a bit of difference. I was actually in fear for my life, and my skills failed in the face of my opponent's utter <u>commitment</u>. He chased me as I scrambled back across the floor, drove me out of the gym and into a rain storm, and shut the door in my face.

At such moments one faces fundamental choices. Oblivious to the cold and wet, I thought very hard, and decided that I had to fight back. This was a critical decision. It would have been all too easy to dismiss my adversary as a cruel madman and return home to lick my wounds. But in that moment I recognized that I had critical work to do, that my life had value, and that I would do what was required to defend it. Twenty years later, I recognize that this series of decisions marked my graduation into the ranks of true martial artists. Without this fundamental approach, no amount of training will withstand a committed assault.

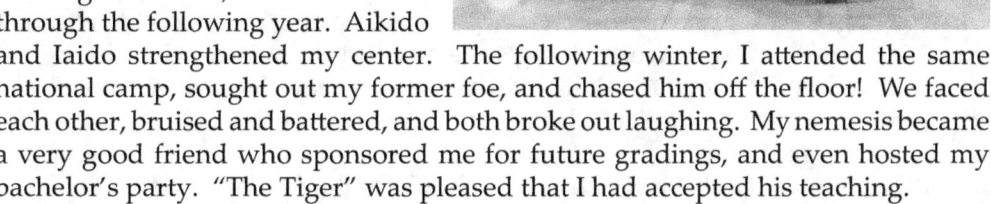

I returned home filled with resolve. Establishing a vigorous training schedule, I stuck to it through the following year. Aikido and Iaido strengthened my center. The following winter, I attended the same national camp, sought out my former foe, and chased him off the floor! We faced each other, bruised and battered, and both broke out laughing. My nemesis became a very good friend who sponsored me for future gradings, and even hosted my bachelor's party. "The Tiger" was pleased that I had accepted his teaching.

Approach the arts and life with whole-hearted commitment is a first step to achieving artistic and personal success. My sword teacher, Eura Kazunori

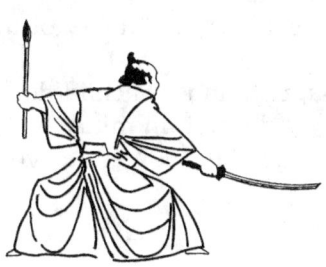

Sensei, says that the primary requirement in Japanese swordsmanship is "show heart." The same is true of Shodo. When I pick up a brush these days, it is the same as if I am holding a sword. I engage all my senses and abilities before attempting the simplest of strokes, and the results are highly rewarding.

To express artistry and power with a brush requires a measure of commitment similar to that required in a martial arts contest. As you increase skill, you will also expand your powers of perception. As you practice Shodo's basic strokes, strive to remain relaxed and focused. You'll be pleasantly surprised at how much more the brush can be controlled when you are comfortable. It strikes me as truly remarkable how an activity as simple as brushing characters reveals human potential. The brush is a sensitive tool. Although your first attempts may be hindered by preconceptions and a certain lack of experience, **don't be discouraged**. Engage the art of Shodo with sincerity and a spirit of playfulness, and you will ultimately be successful!

The Discovery of Self-Mastery

Both children and adults love to paint. Most westerners are unfamilar with the deep meanings of *kanji* characters, but we are still drawn to the mysteriousness of their shapes and the dynamic contrast between black ink and white paper. We are attracted to the sinuous power expressed by brushes motivated by mind-body coordination. I am continually surprised by the excitement and pleasure of students, from young to old, who come to 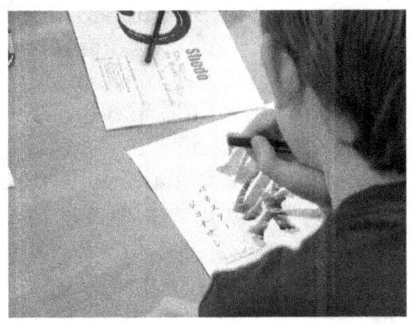 Shodo classes keen to experience this fascinating aspect of Japanese culture. It is more surprising to my Japanese friends, who are amazed that the challenges of brush writing are of any interest to westerners.

One of my greatest delights as a teacher occurs when a new student discovers a heightened sense of their own potential through an encounter with the great Japanese martial or cultural arts traditions. There are moments when a light bulb appears to go off in a student's mind. Sometimes it is only the faint glow of beginning comprehension. At other times their discovery of self-mastery explodes into incandescence.

One of the greatest attributes of the Japanese people is their propensity for polishing every discipline to the level of high art. Even a task as seemingly simple as sweeping a walkway is approached with intensity and a responsible attitude. Anything worth doing, is worth doing superbly. It is no wonder that the simple communication and language skills of brush writing have been developed into a discipline that cultivates spirit, illuminates human potential, and facilitates the achievement of self-mastery.

Practicing the twelve basic strokes of Shodo will help you to develop a high degree of hand-eye coordination and the capacity to paint calmly and surely with your whole being. If you also pay attention to the correct coordination of mind and body, you will release your innate potential and be able to express internal energy through your brush. Even simple strokes can express the totality of the human experience.

As you get started, it is enough to cultivate the happy mind of a child doing the next best thing to finger-painting. Self-mastery will develop in mind, body, and spirit to the extent that you enjoy practicing to achieve it. So get out your brushes, and have some fun!

Practice Sample Worksheets

The following pages feature worksheets illustrating Shodo's twelve basic brush strokes, as well as *kanji* characters in *kaisho, gyosho*, and *sosho* styles, and compositions for multi-character vertical phrases and four-character idioms. A sufficient investment made in the practice of basics will help you to brush complete characters with a minimum of frustration. Always remember to extend energy calmly from your center and through the brush. Painting should be physically relaxing, even though you will have to concentrate a lot, too.

36

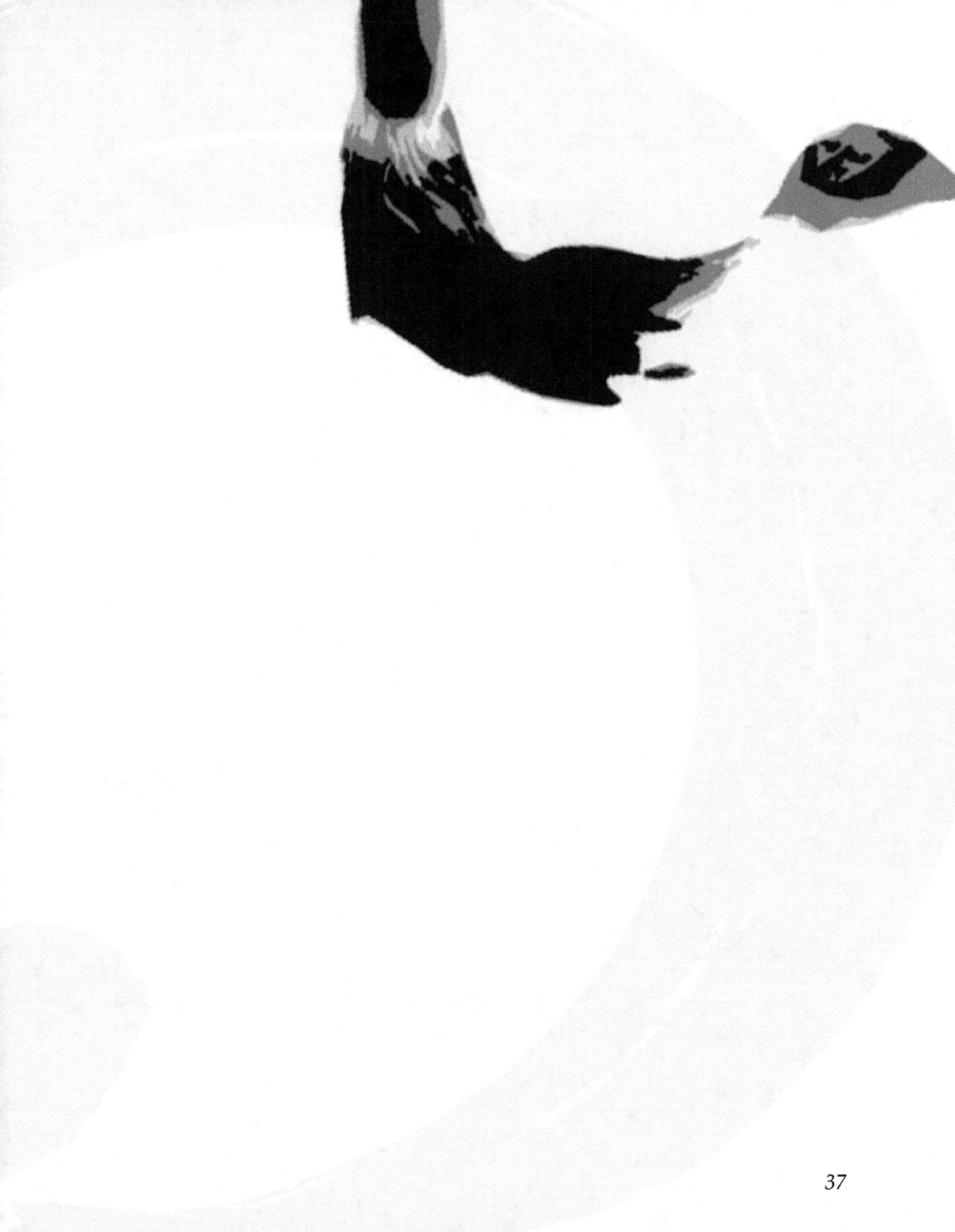

Part 2

Practice Samples

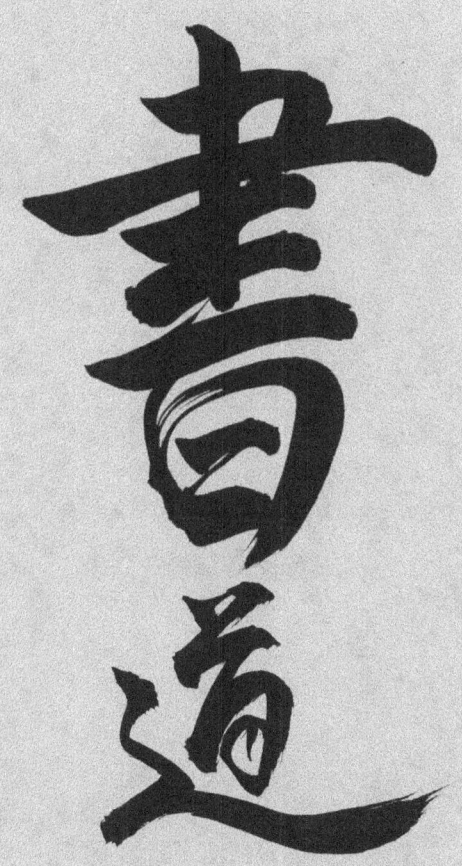

AiShinKai **Publications**
Self-Mastery in Daily Life
www.aishinkai.com

The Twelve Basic Strokes of *Shodo* Brush Calligraphy

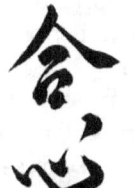

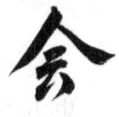

Ai Shin Kai Harmonious Heart Association

Basic Principles of Shodo: Brush Calligraphy

- Create a Calm Center
- Be Comfortably Relaxed
- Practice Dependable Posture
- Unify Body, Mind and Spirit
- Hold the Brush Vertically
- Stop-Start-Stop
- Concentrate Through the Brush
- Practice with Diligence and Patience
- Be Attentive to Positive and Negative Shapes
- Combine Large and Small Characters
- Combine Thick and Thin Strokes
- One Nijimi, One Kasure

Dr. Jonathan Bannister, *Founder & President*

*B*efore trying to draw whole characters, you wil need to develop a few basic skills in brush handling. Twelve basic strokes form the building blocks of Japanese brush calligraphy, with horizontal and vertical lines being the most elemental. I will explain how to make these strokes so that you can create lines that are balanced and infused with visual energy.

Important Basics

Calmness - Practice in a quiet place, and cultivate a calm center from which to motivate your calligraphy.

Relax - Let go of any excess tension in body and mind. Lower your shoulders. Excess tension causes stiff and unnatural strokes.

Posture - Take extra care to sit correctly and move the brush with your whole arm. Extend from your center, through the arm, to brush, to paper.

Unify Body, Mind and Spirit - Paint with confidence. Even technically incorrect strokes can express beauty if executed with conviction.

Train your eye - Hold the stroke or character lightly in your mind, and be conscious of the direction of the brush, anchor points, alignment on the page, overall shapes, and ink gradations that you wish to create.

HORIZONLAL LINES - *Yokoga* (横画)

It seems so simple. Yet in many traditional Shodo schools, beginning students might be required to practice this basic stroke for months. Just like in martial arts training, basic skills are the building blocks for everything that comes after. Aikido students practice to refine basic footwork, Iaido students diligently practice to master basic sword handling, and Kyudo practitioners train in the eight basics movements of the *hassetsu* (八節). Similarly, Shodo practitioners continually refine the intricacies of horizontal and vertical lines. As a beginner, I found it extraordinarily difficult - even mystifying - to create the well-balanced lines required to make beautiful Shodo characters. Only practice hasmade it possible for me to draw their shapes correctly with any sort of dependability.

Horizontal lines are always drawn left-to-right, and the brush must be held vertically. There may even be a slight tilt of the handle away from you. Pay close attention to your posture so that you can float the brush up and down, expressing *ton-dou-ton* (遯動遯), the natural rhythm of stop-move-stop. The finished shape should resemble a bone, or a segment of bamboo.

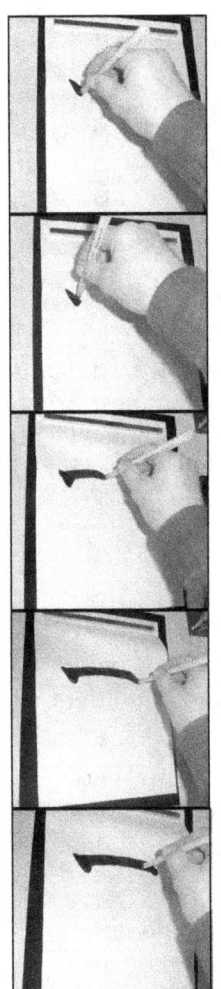

Step 1
Load the brush by dipping it into the well of the ink stone, then form the bristles into a sharp tip by twirling the bristles as you brush away excess ink on the "land." Carefully place the brush on the paper, tip first, taking care not to move the tip as you lower the bristles on a 45° angle until the full length of the bristles touches the paper.

Step 2
Push the handle slightly away from you, taking care not to move the bristles, but lifting the back of the bristles (bottom of the stroke) to make a *dango* (団子). The line needs this bulge to visually anchor the stroke to the paper.

Step 3
Use a floating feeling in your elbow to gently lift the brush as you stroke smoothly and naturally to the right. The motion should be made resolutely, with a sense of forming a bridge from the first resting position to the next.

Step 4
Complete the stroke with the bristles in full contact with the paper. Pause briefly to allow the ink to absorb.

Step 5
Carefully lift the back of the bristles (bottom of the stroke) to form an anchor point, and retrace your path carefully to the left, lifting the brush away from the paper to form a smooth edge to the right end of the stroke. If you do not do this step, the edge will often be ragged and unattractive.

Vertical Lines - *Tatega* (縦画) - Basic Stroke #3

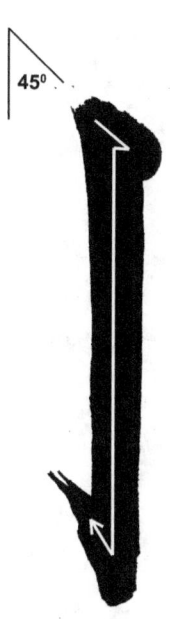

45°

Of the three vertical lines - basic strokes #2, #3 and #4 - I have selected the third because it is slightly more complex. I find its execution interesting and enjoyable. Vertical strokes are written top to bottom. Just as characters flow down the paper like water cascading down a mountain, vertical lines should flow smoothly down into your center. Observe the principle of *ton-dou-ton* (遯動遯), or stop-move-stop, just as for horizontal lines.

For years I found vertical strokes difficult to keep straight, smooth, and vertical. These strokes can be well-brushed using a straight downward "cutting" feeling, similar to the large overhead cut in swordsmanship called *kirioroshi* (切り下ろし). Begin with an outwards extension from your center to the paper, then brush deliberately downwards to rejoin your center at the end of the line. To make the smoothest strokes, be calm and relaxed.

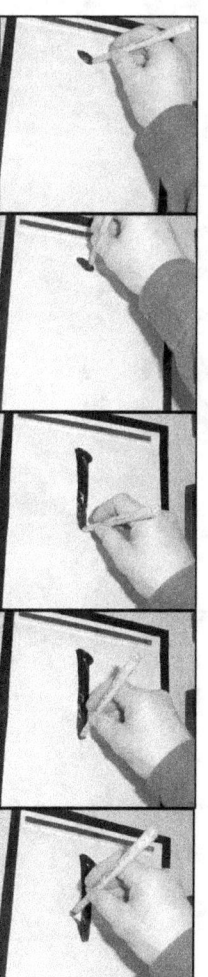

Step 1 (same as with horizontal lines)
Load the brush by dipping it into the well of the ink stone, then form the bristles into a sharp tip by twirling the bristles as you brush away excess ink on the "land." Carefully place the brush on the paper tip first, taking care not to move the tip as you lower the bristles on a 45° angle until the full length of the bristles touches the paper.

Step 2
Push the handle slightly away from you, taking care not to move the bristles, but lifting the back of the bristles (bottom of the stroke) to make a *dango* (団子). The stroke needs to bulge slightly to the right so that the vertical stroke will visually anchor on the paper. The vertical "hangs" off this anchor.

Step 3
A floating feeling in the elbow is used to gently lift the brush as you pull the stroke smoothly and resolutely to your center. Care should be taken to keep the pressure and the width of the stroke as uniform as possible. This will take some practice. If you move too slowly, then - like when riding a bicycle - you will wobble. Gently exhale through the strokes to maintain calmness and relaxation. Be as comfortable as possible: any unnatural tension in either body or mind will make your strokes uncertain.

Step 4
Complete the stroke with the bristles in full contact with the paper. Pause briefly to allow ink to absorb.

Step 5
Playfully lift off the bristles to the left at an angle of 45°. This forms a dynamic tail that is very attractive when properly balanced with the length of the stroke.

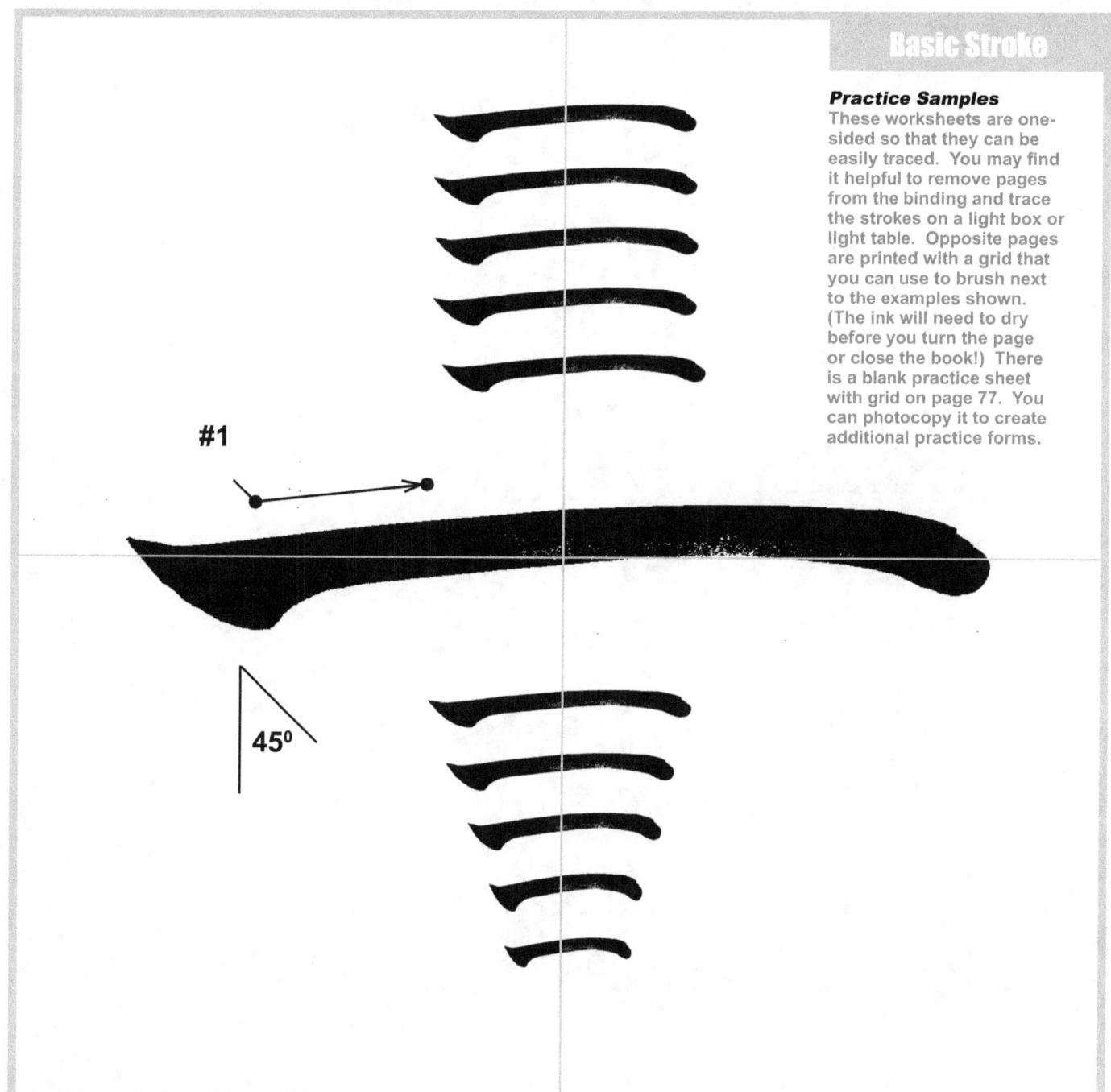

#1

45⁰

Shodo: *Brush Calligraphy*
Basic Stroke #1
Yokoga (横画) - Horizontal Lines ("Bone" or "Bamboo")

Hold the brush vertically. Deliberately lay the bristles on a 45° diagonal, starting on the left side, then lift slightly and draw to the right, finish by pressing, pausing, an lifting back. First, try to draw parallel lines of the same length; then experiment with increasing and decreasing stroke lengths.

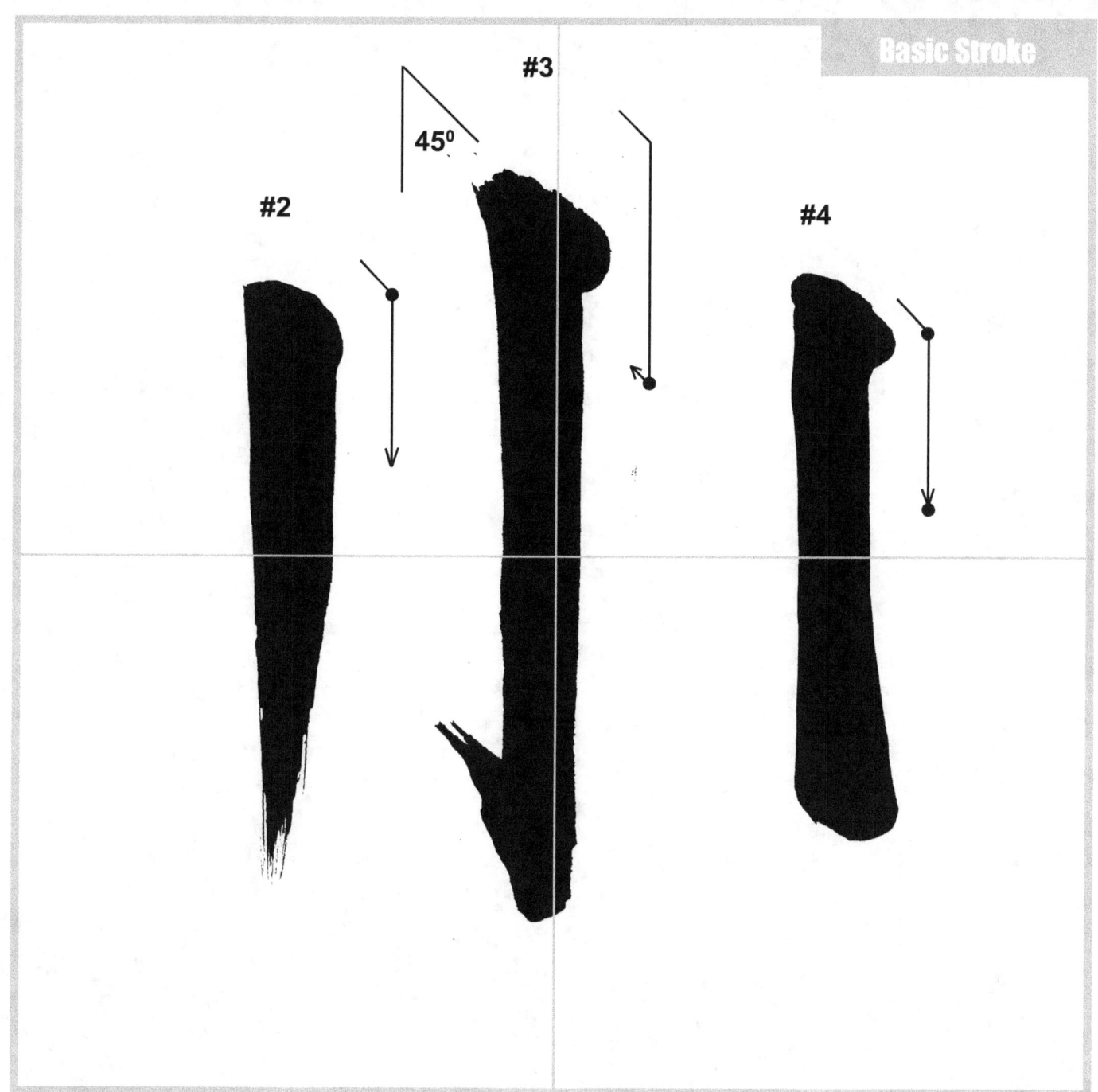

Shodo: *Brush Calligraphy*
Basic Strokes #2, #3, and #4
Tatega (縦画) - Vertical Lines ("Standing Lines")

Lay the bristles on a 45° diagonal at the top, then draw down as if the ink were running downhill: (#2) gradually lift to cause the ink to "trail"; (#3) pause at the bottom, then slowly lift the bristles to form a rising tail to the left; (#4) draw down and pause to allow ink to soak in, forming a *dango* (団子), or dumpling.

AiShinKai
Self-Mastery in Daily Life
Edmonds, WA
www.aishinkai.com

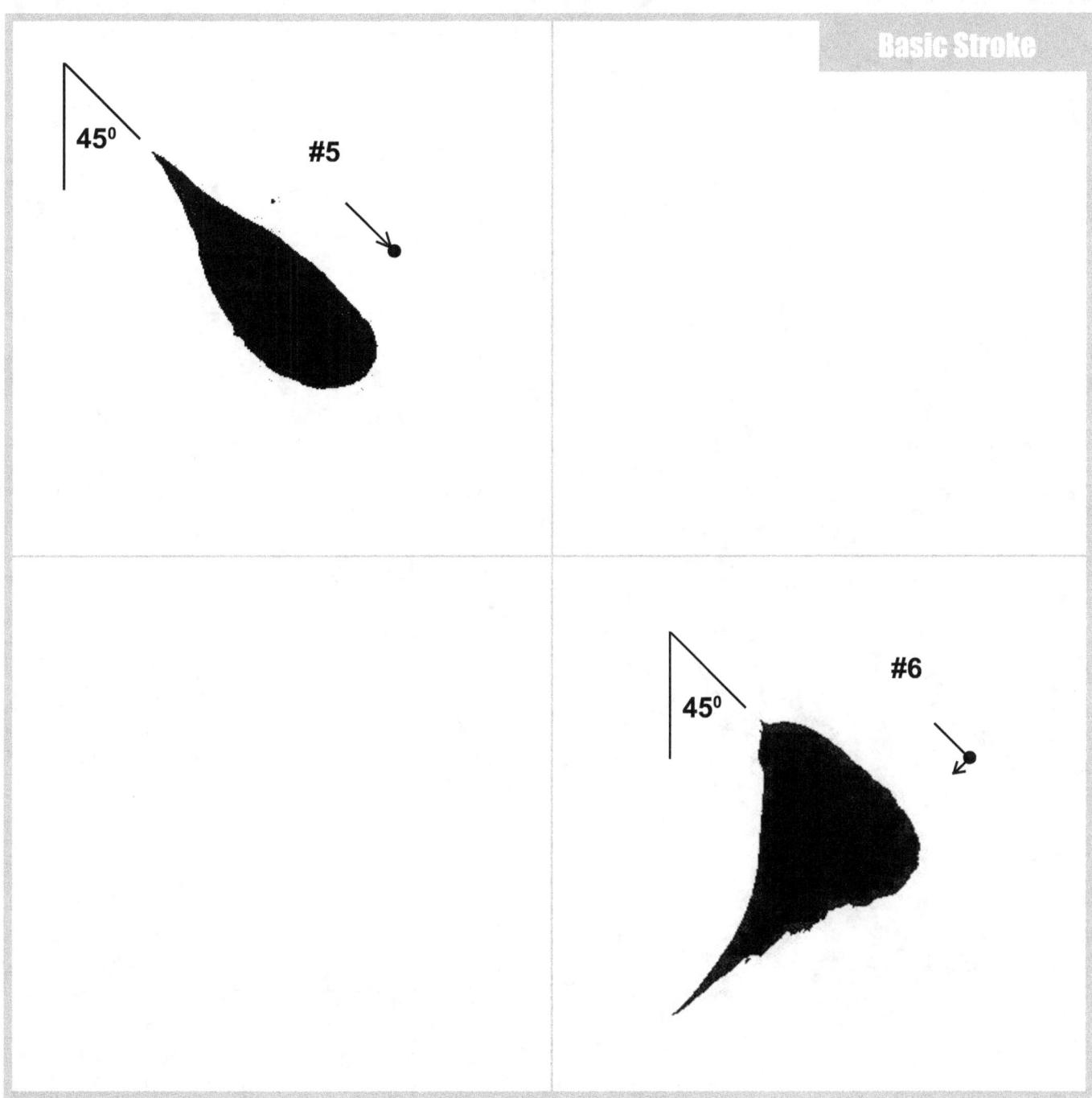

45⁰ #5

45⁰ #6

Shodo: *Brush Calligraphy*
Basic Strokes #5 & #6
Ten (点) - Dots ("Raindrop" & "Barb")

Lay the bristles on a 45° diagonal starting with the tip at the top left: (#5) barely moving the tip, press the bristles down to form the raindrop; (#6) lift down and to the left to make a barb.

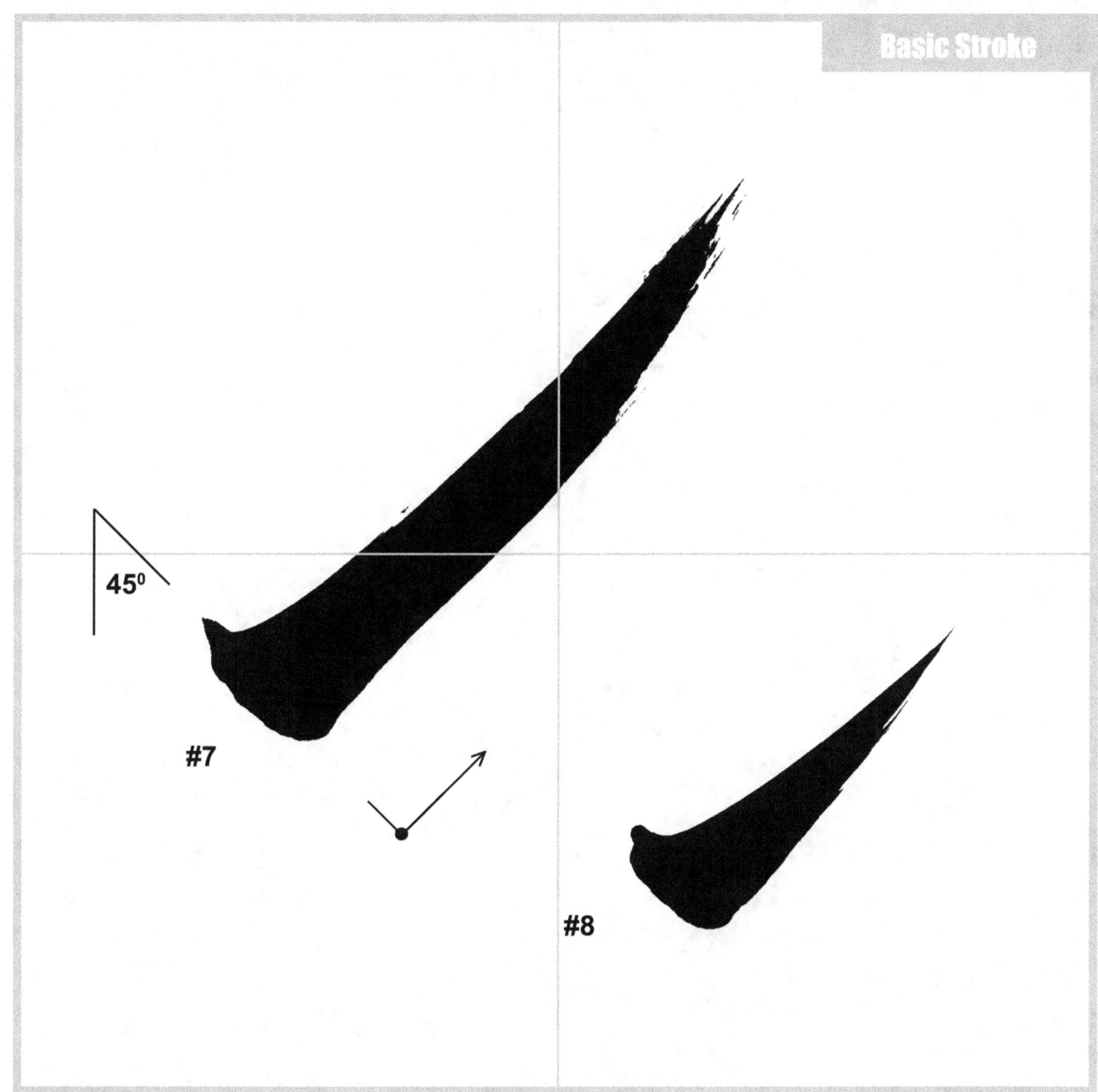

45⁰

#7

#8

Shodo: *Brush Calligraphy*
Basic Strokes #7 and #8
Katana (刀) and *Kodachi* (小太刀) - Long and Short Swords
Lay the bristles on a 45° diagonal at the bottom left, then draw slowly upwards to the right as if the ink were floating gently on a cloud, lifting gradually to form the sharp tail.

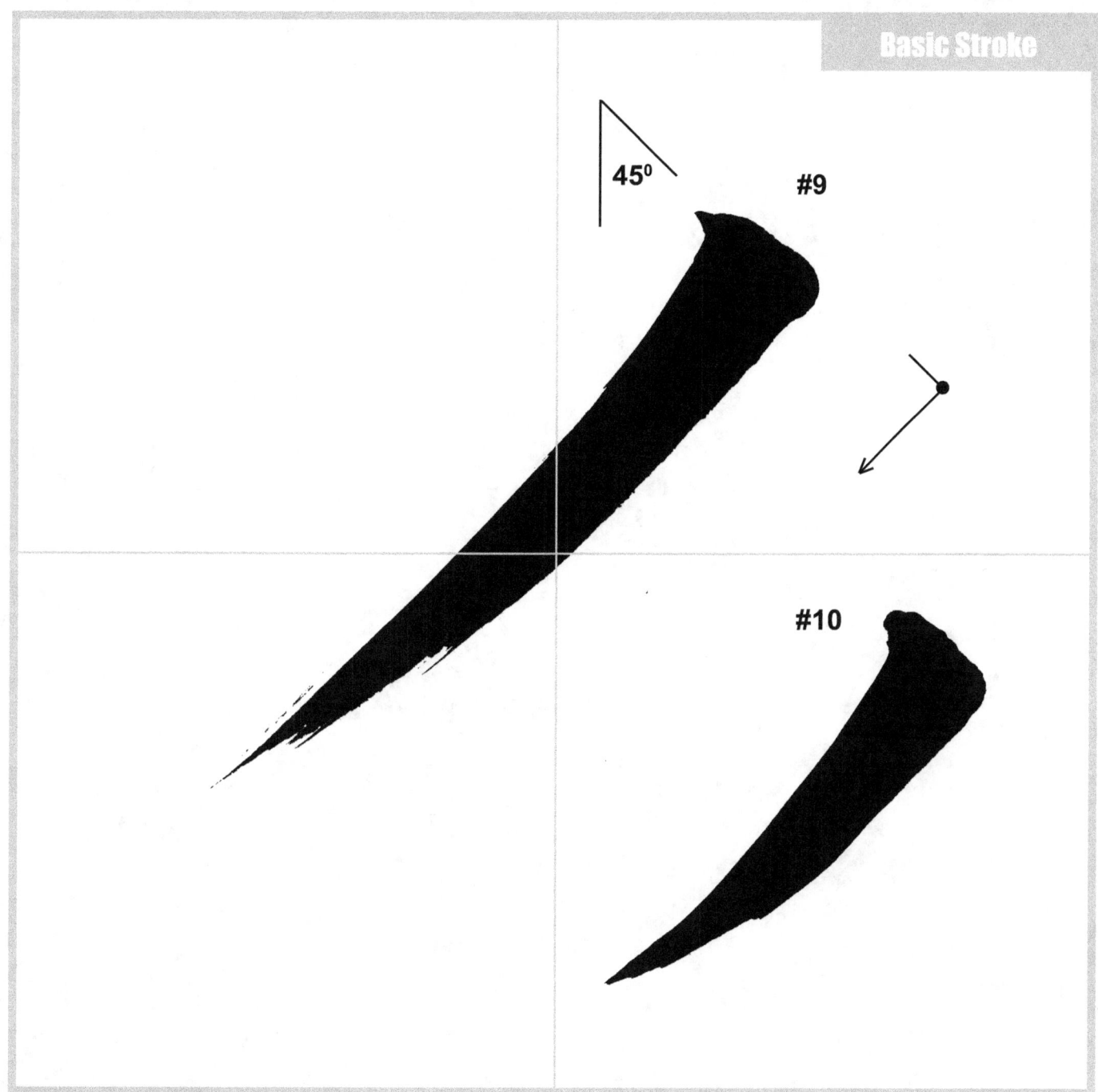

45⁰

#9

#10

Shodo: *Brush Calligraphy*
Basic Strokes #9 and #10
Kesa (袈裟) and *Ryuu no Tsume* (龍の爪) - "Collar" (stole of Buddhist priest) and "Dragon Claw"

Lay the bristles on a 45° diagonal at the top right, then draw slowly downwards to the right as if the ink were flowing gently downhill, lifting gradually to form the sharp tail.

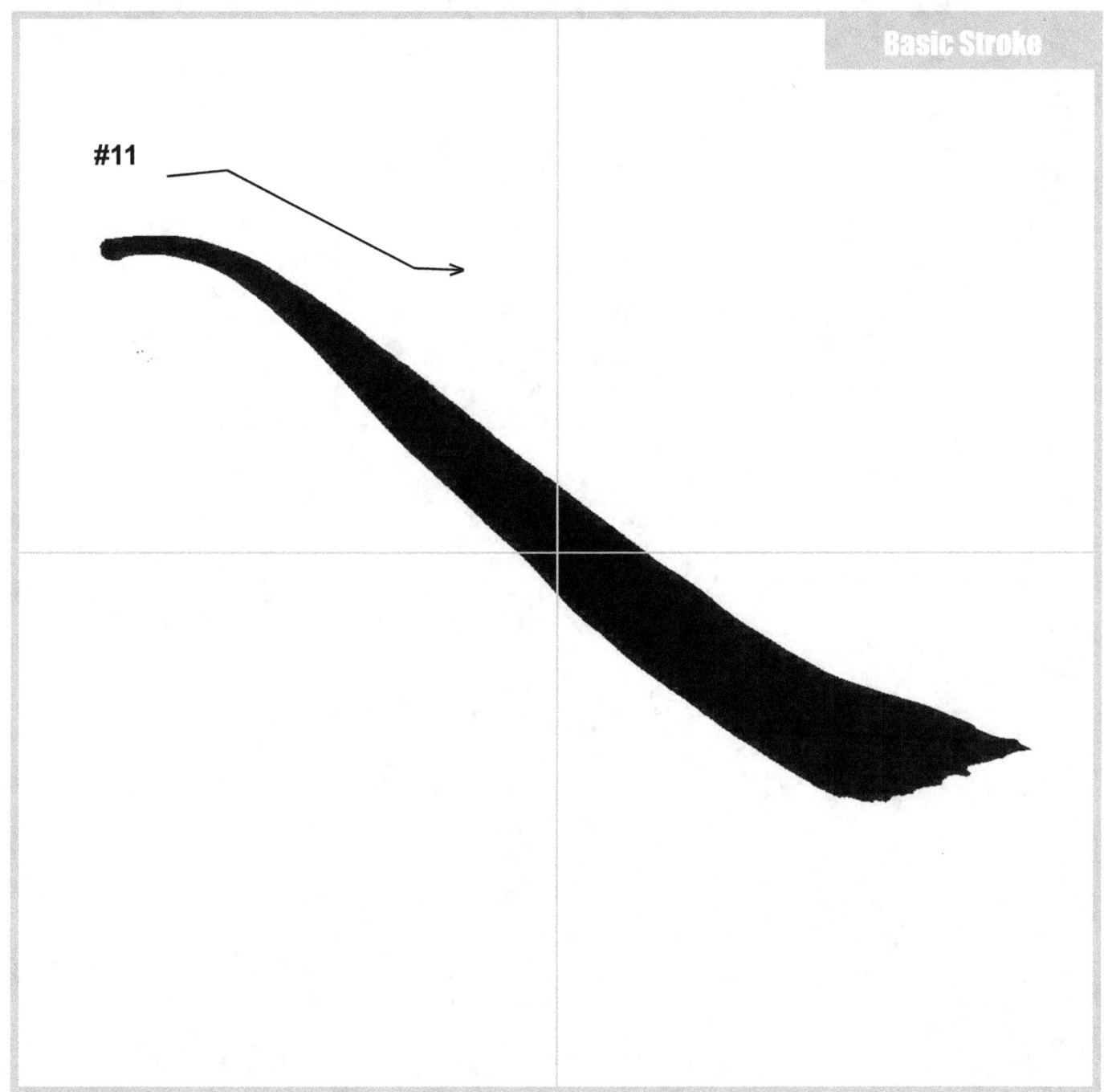

#11

Shodo: *Brush Calligraphy*
Basic Stroke #11
Hera (篦) Spatula - ("Slide")

Touch lightly, top left. Gradually accelerate down to the right, gently adding pressure to thicken the line. Slow down slightly as you approach the bottom; carefully lift the brush while slowly turning the bristles clockwise to form the tail.

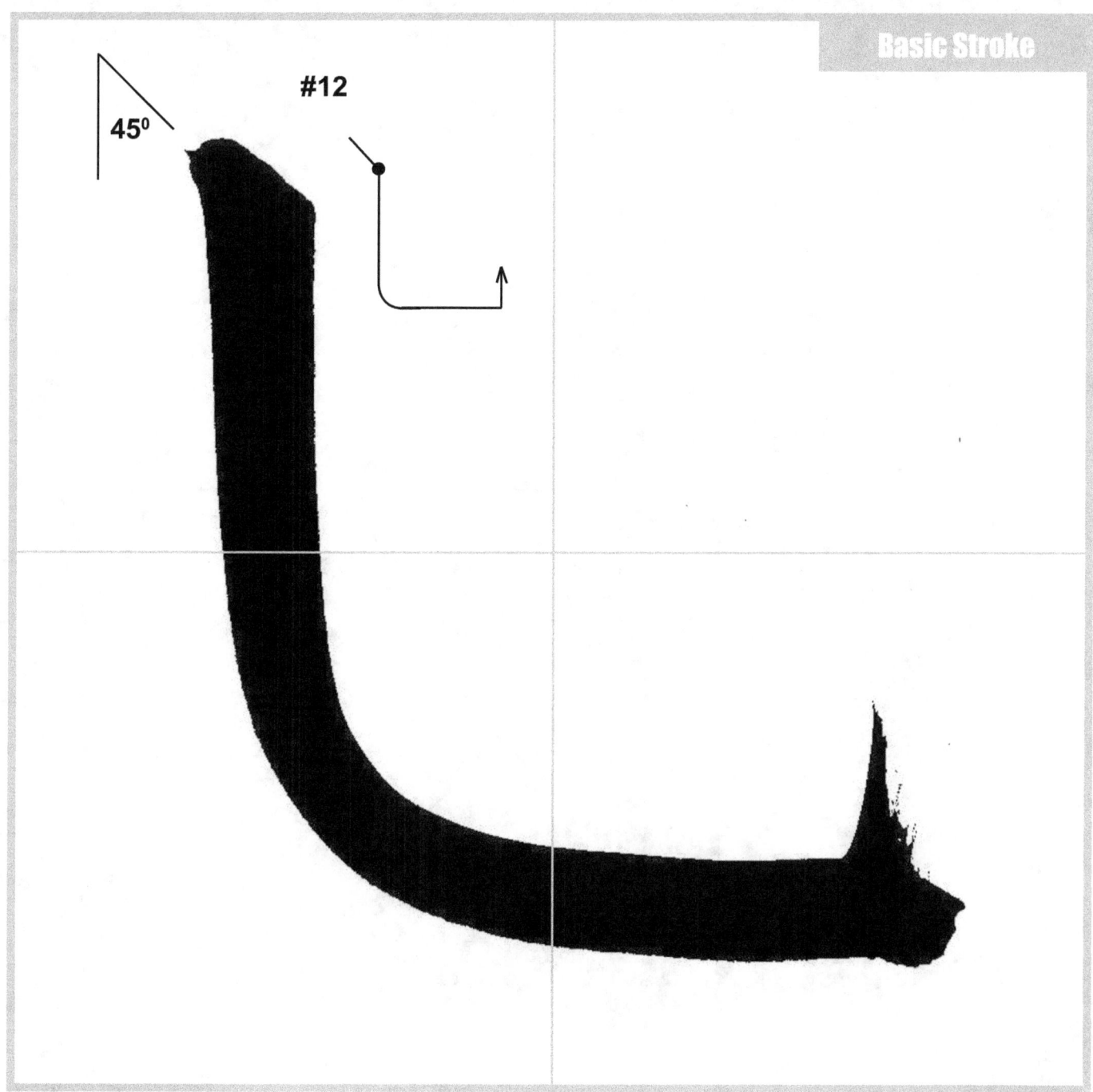

Shodo: *Brush Calligraphy*
Basic Stroke #9
Tensetsu (転折) - Continuous Line ("Fishhook")

Lay the bristles on a 45° diagonal at the top, then draw down as if the ink were running downhill. Without hesitation, turn to the right at the bottom; pause for an instant, and then lift the bristles to form the tail.

Numbers on each line indicate the stroke order. Use these to visualize the path the brush will make on the paper. This will help you to compose and balance the character, and will eventually encourage cursive, dynamic brushing.

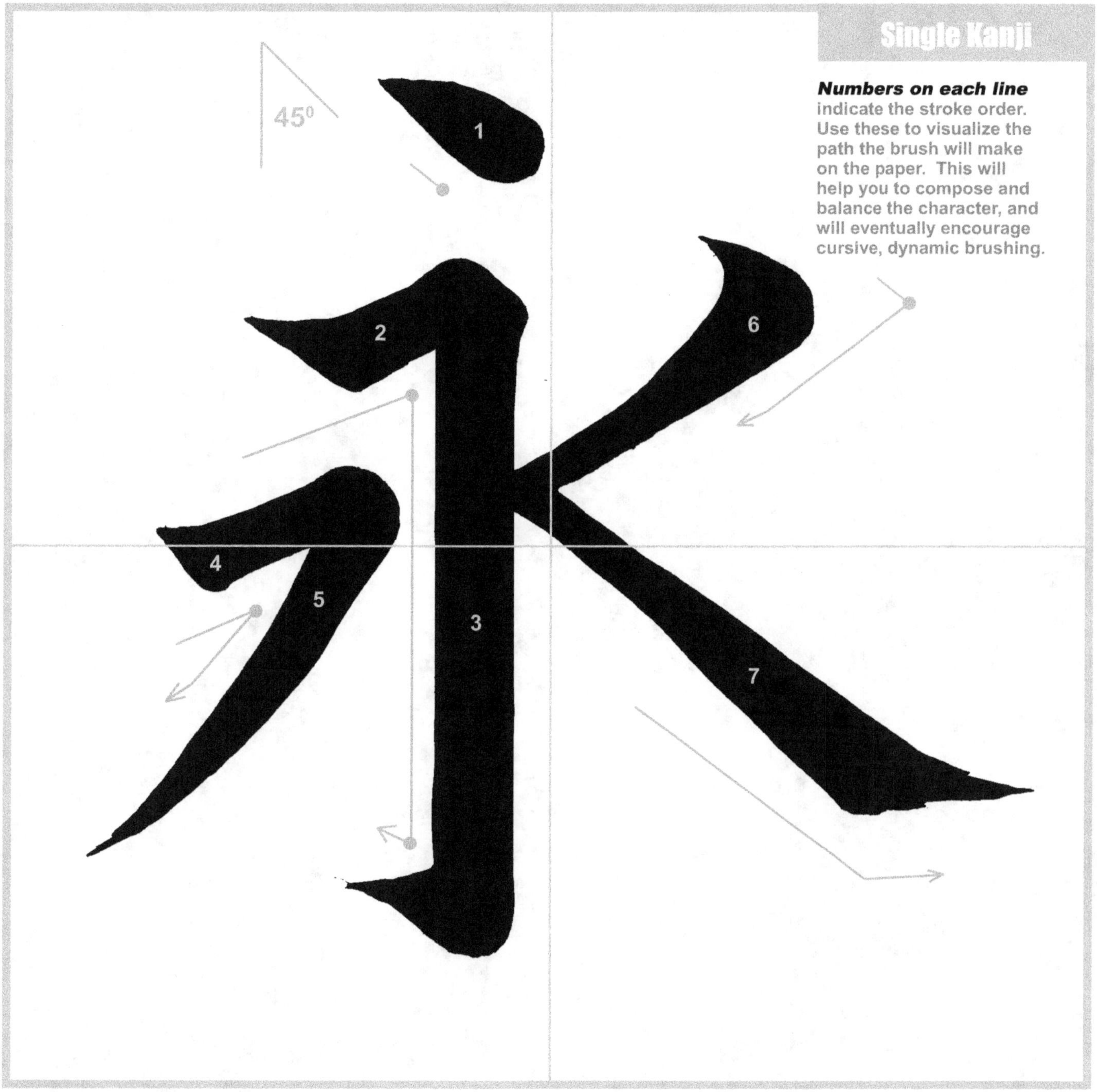

45⁰

1

2

6

4

5

3

7

Shodo: *Brush Calligraphy*
Kanji - *Kaisho* (block) style
Ei (永) - Forever

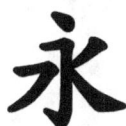

A practical standard, this *kanji* contains most of the essential brush strokes used to draw other characters, from the simplest to the most complex.

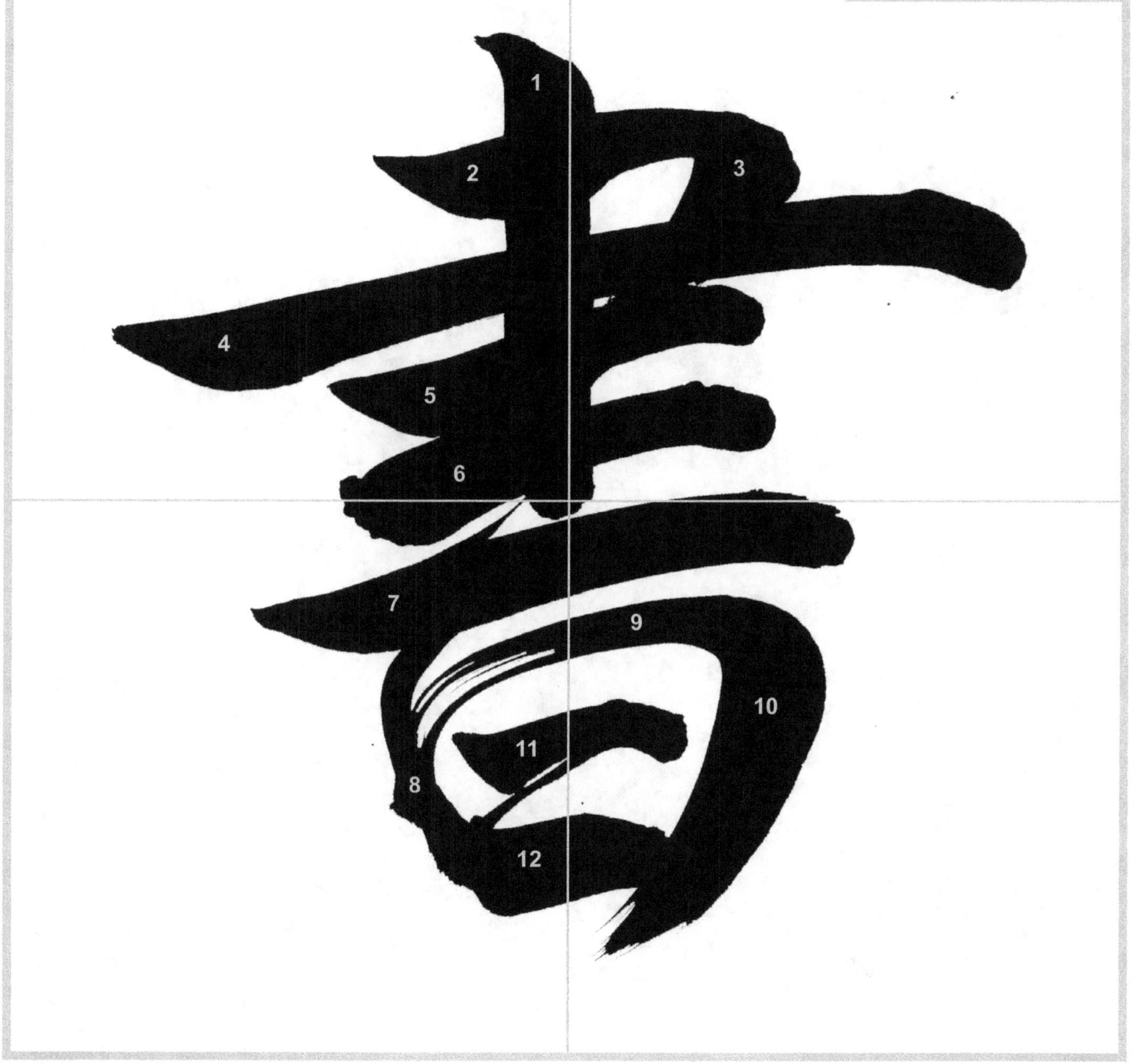

Shodo: *Brush Calligraphy*
Kanji - *Gyosho* (cursive) style
Sho (書) - Writing

One of the hardest characters to paint: see if you can keep it balanced.

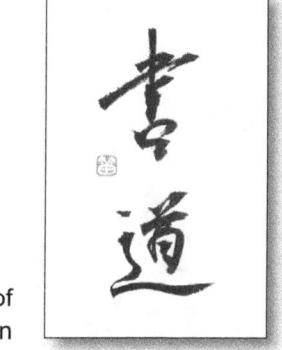

A fine *gyosho* rendition of
"Shodo" by calligrapher Feri Kun

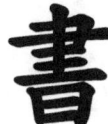

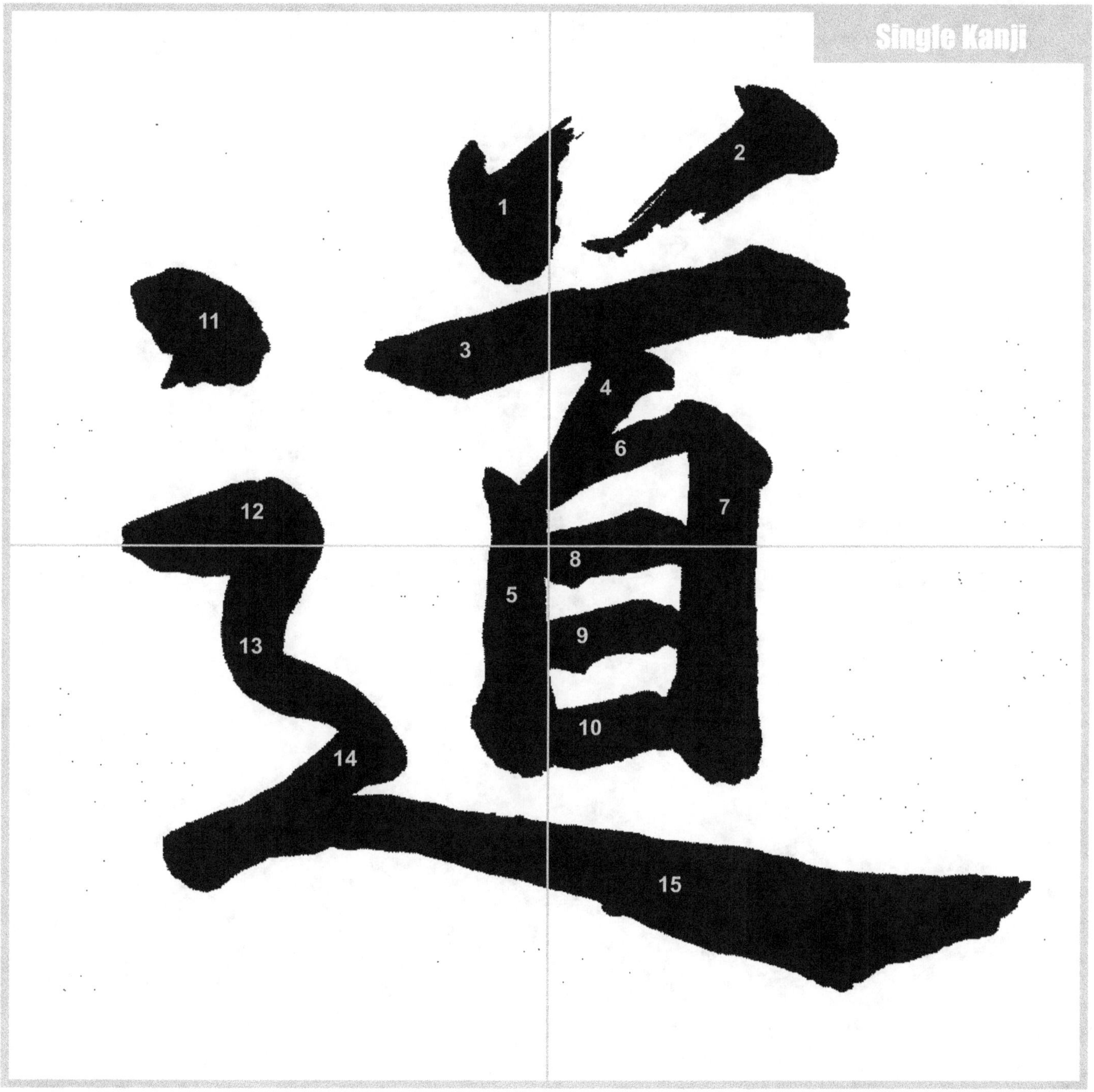

道

Shodo: *Brush Calligraphy*
Kanji - *Kaisho* (block) style
Do (道) - The Way

A road, a path, a spiritual journey. Can also be read "*Tao*" or "*Michi*."
Represents a monk walking an endless road.

道

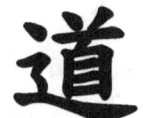

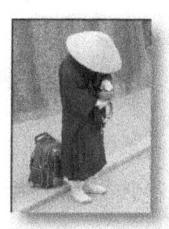

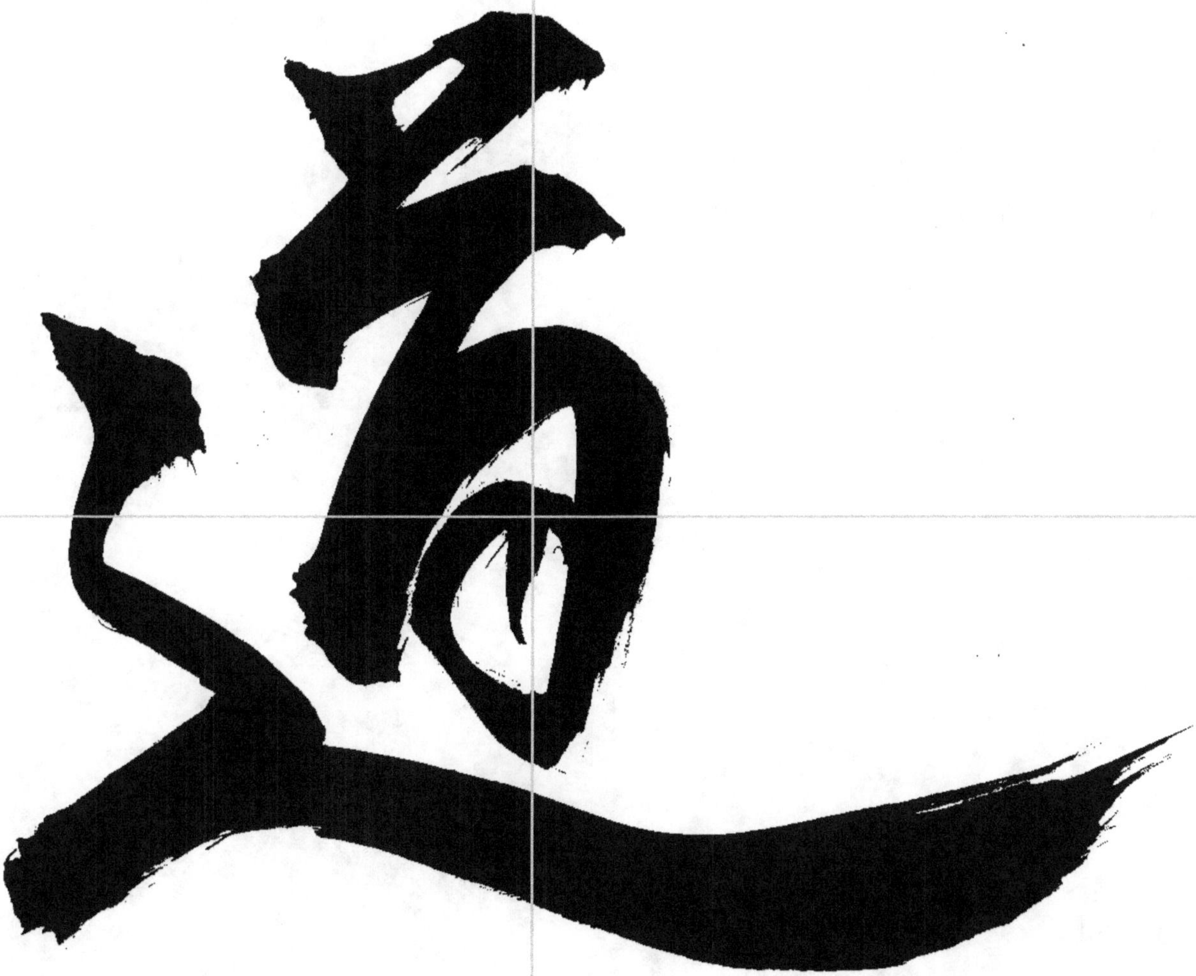

道

Shodo: *Brush Calligraphy*
Kanji - *Gyosho* (semi cursive) style
Do (道) - The Way

A road, a path, a spiritual journey. Can also be read "*Tao*" or "*Michi*."
Represents a monk walking an endless road..

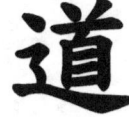

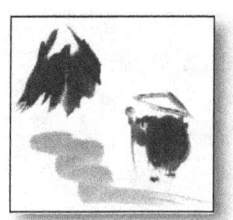

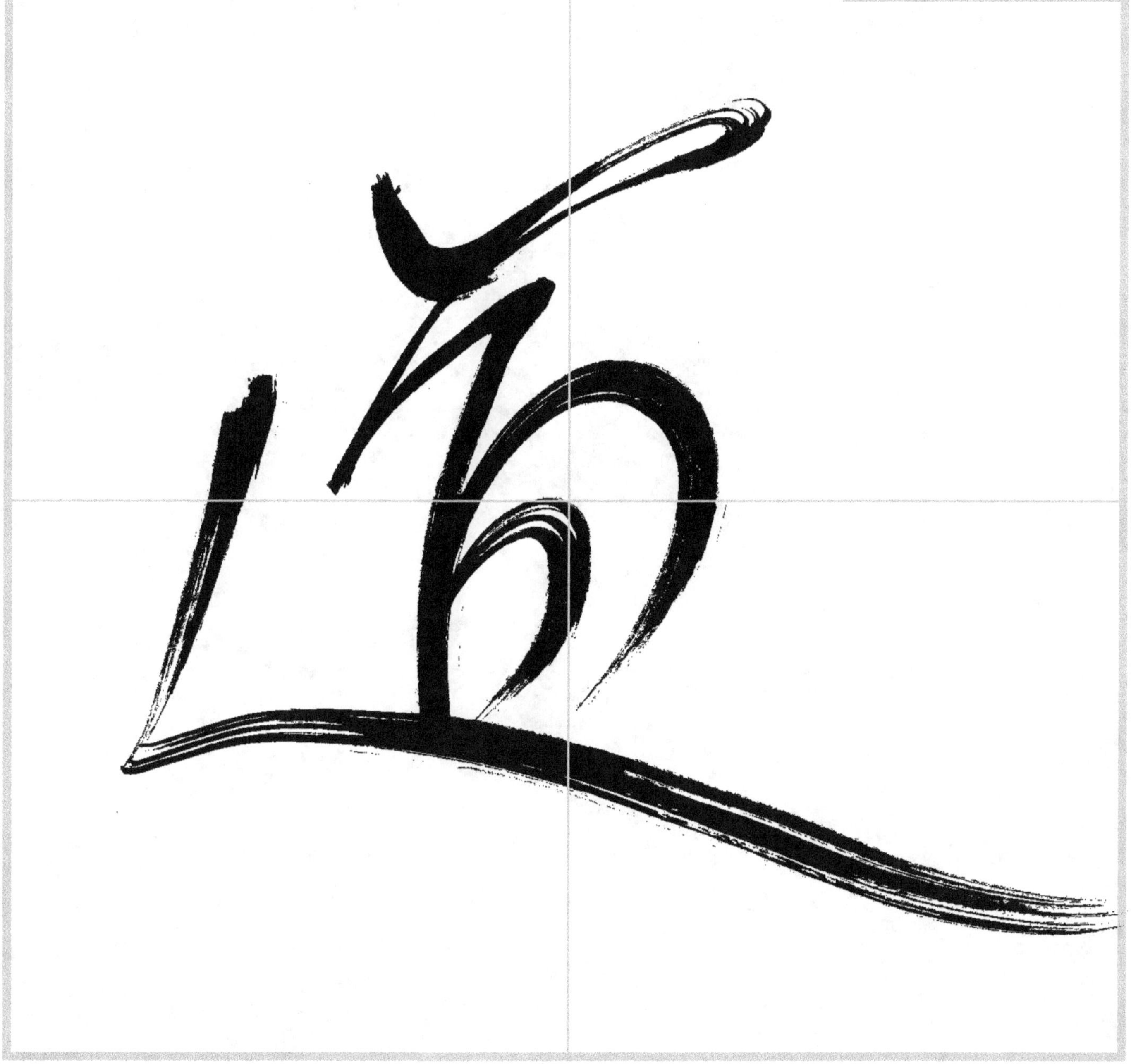

Shodo: *Brush Calligraphy*
Kanji - *Sosho* (full cursive) style
Do (道) - The Way

道

A road, a path, a spiritual journey. Can also be read "*Tao*" or "*Michi*."
Represents a monk walking an endless road.

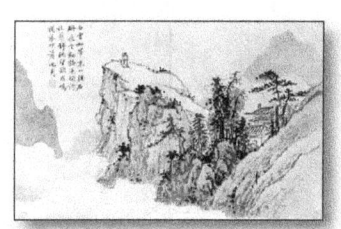

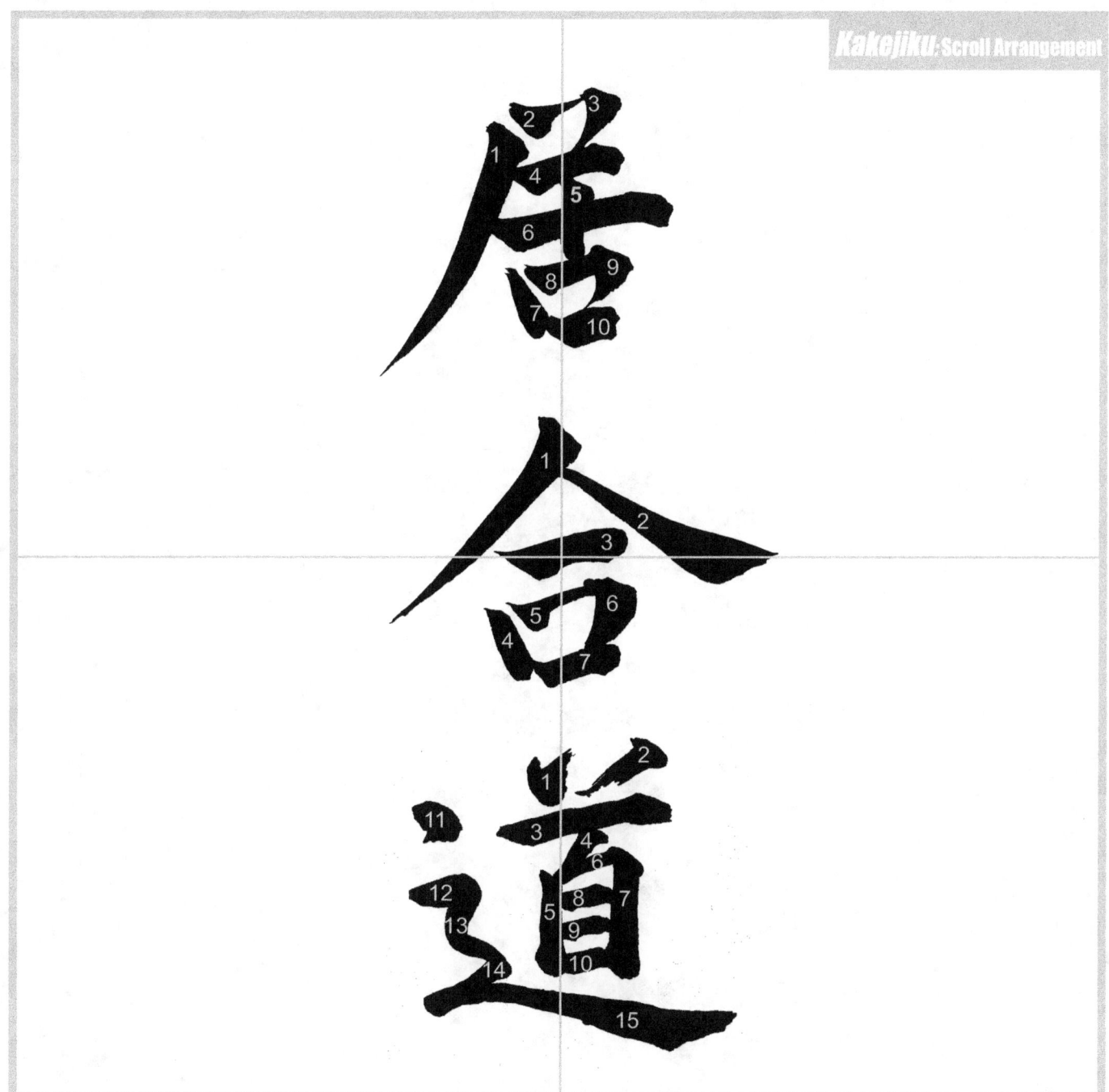

Shodo: *Brush Calligraphy*
Kanji - *Kaisho* style
Iaido (居合道) - Way of Harmonious Posture

居合道

Art of quick-draw swordsmanship practiced by millions of people
world-wide. The kanji *i* (居) means posture/position coupled with inner
motivation, *ai* (合) is "harmony," and *do* (道) indicates "spiritual path."

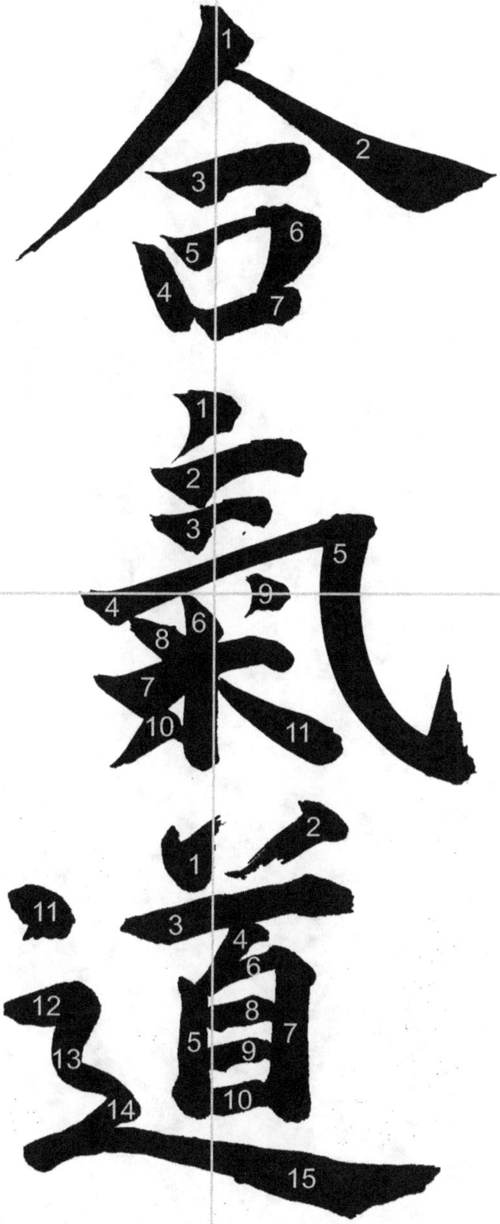

合氣道

Shodo: *Brush Calligraphy*
Kanji - *Kaisho* style
Aikido (合氣道) - Way of Spiritual Harmony

合氣道

A profoundly non-violent martial art founded by Morihei Ueshiba in 1927.
Ai (合) represents a "mouth" and a "roof:" we speak and live as one; *ki* (氣) is "spiritual energy," rice cooking over fire; *do* (道) is "spiritual path," a monk walks an endles road.

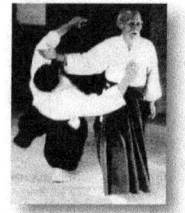

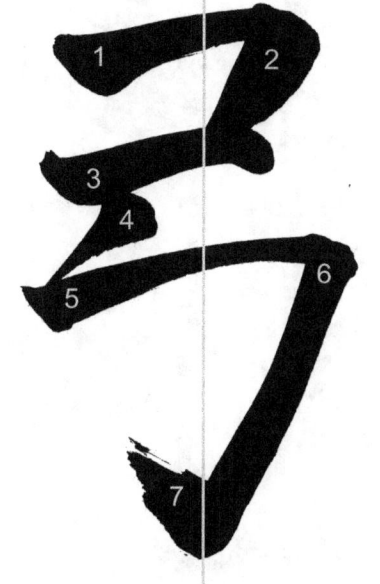

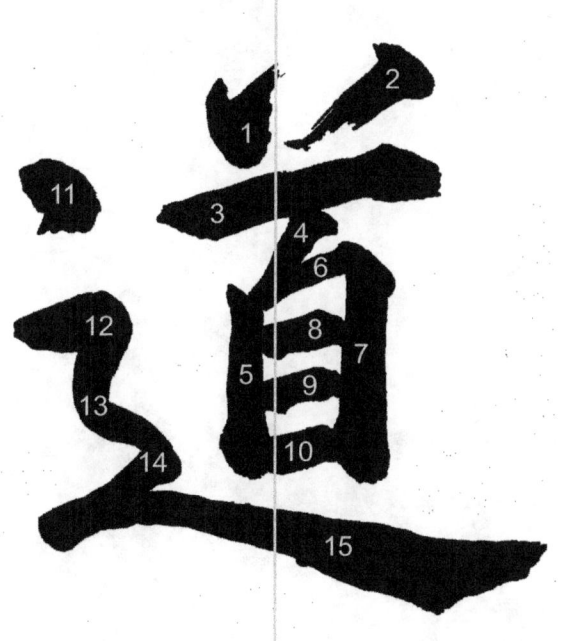

Shodo: *Brush Calligraphy*
Kanji - *Kaisho* style
Kyudo (弓道) - Way of the Bow

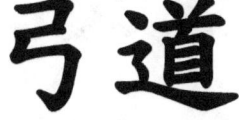

A modern martial discipline devoted to spiritual development through use of the traditional Japanese bow. The kanji *kyu* (弓) is derived from the shape of a bow and arrow.

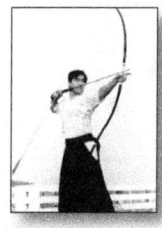

73

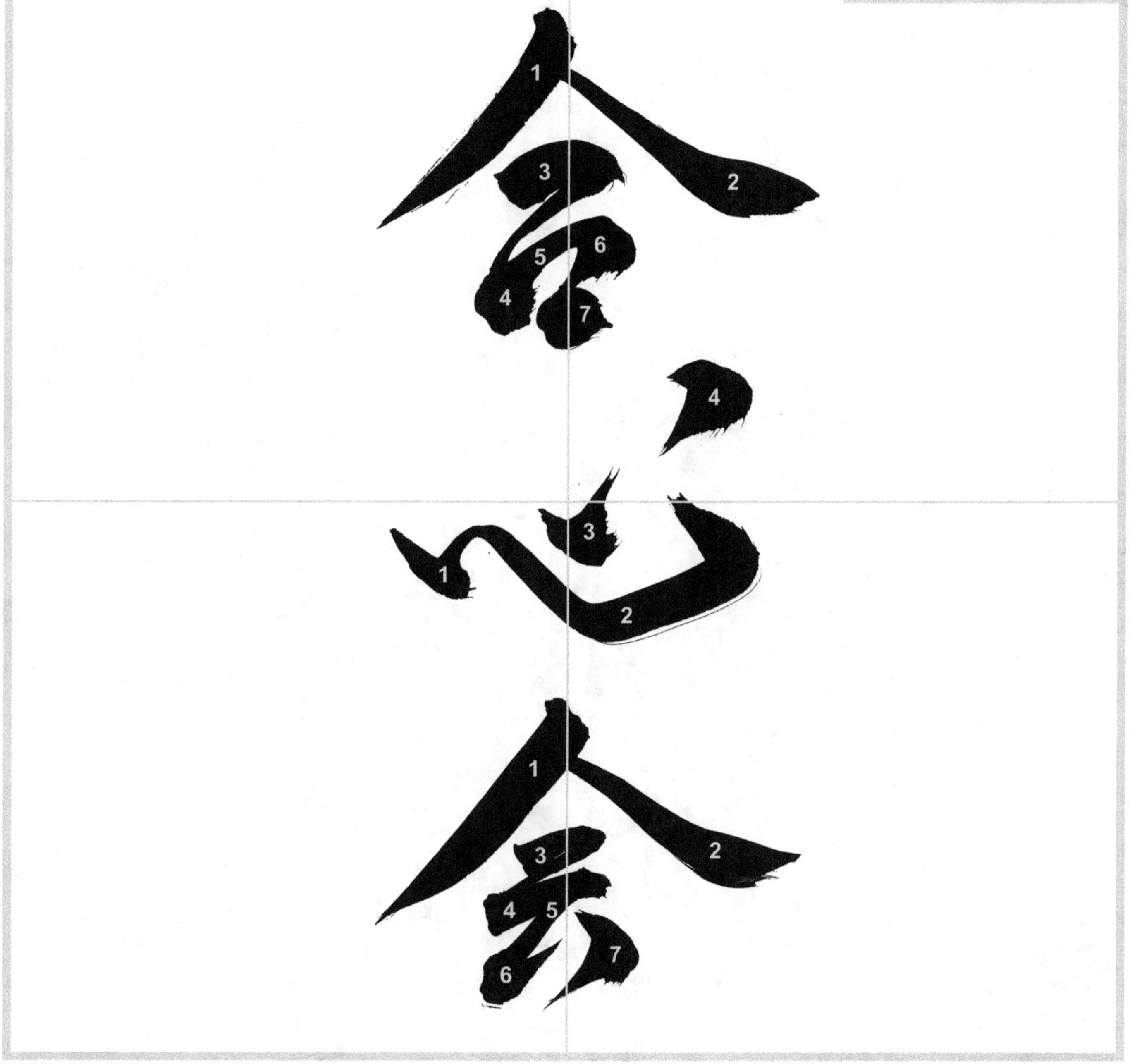

Shodo: *Brush Calligraphy*
Kanji - *Gyosho* style
AiShinKai (合心会) - Harmonious Heart Association

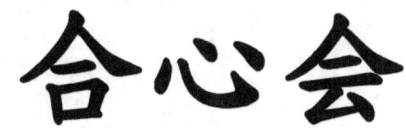

A membership organization devoted to helping others achieve self-mastery and peak performance in all aspects of daily life through the study of Japanese martial and cultural arts. *Ai* (合) represents a "mouth" and a "roof:" to speak and live as one; *shin* (心) is "heart" or "mind;" *kai* (会) is "organization."

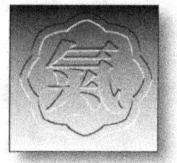

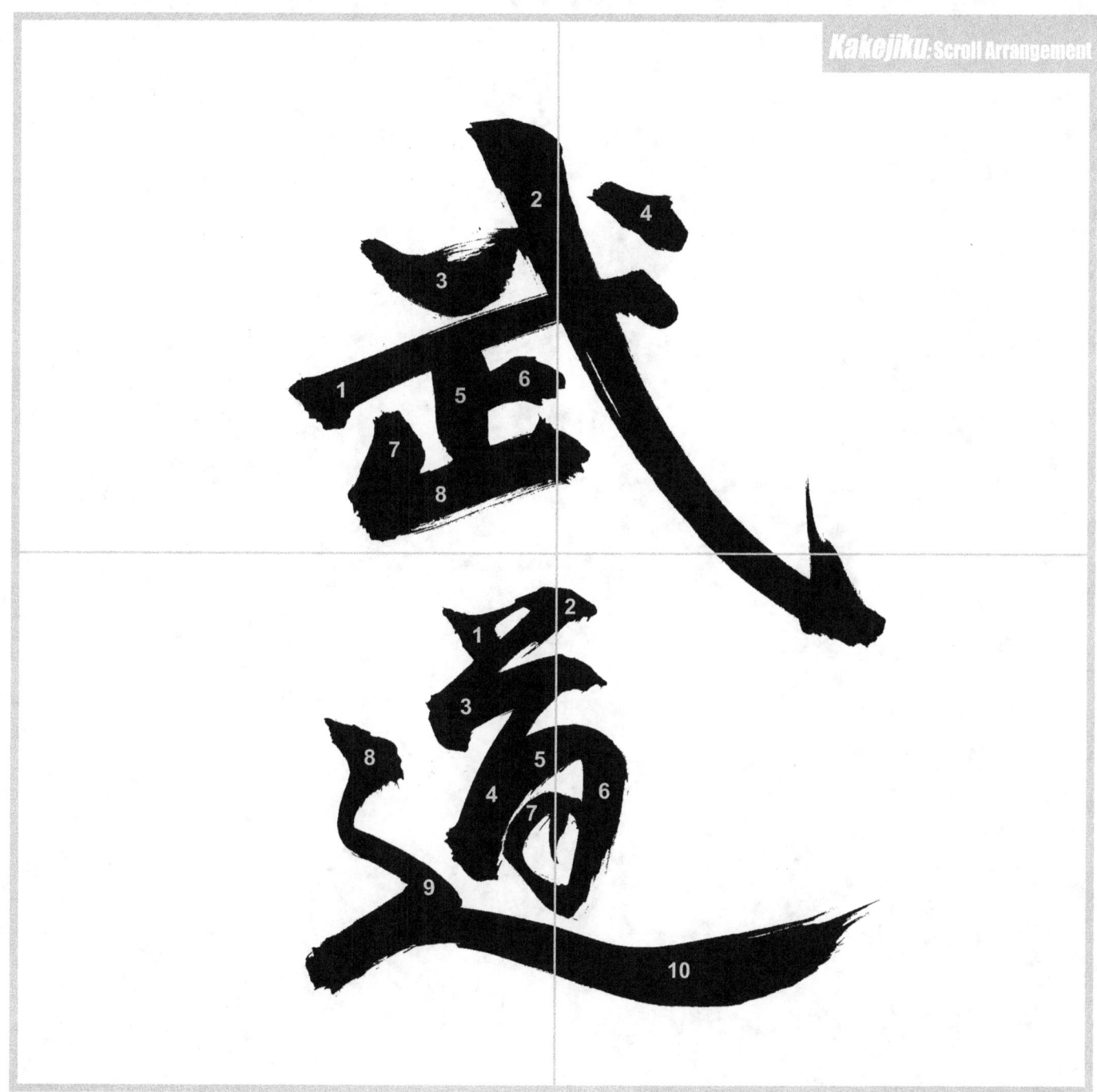

Shodo: *Brush Calligraphy*
Kanji - *Gyosho* style
Budo (武道) - Way of Warriors

This term distinguishes Japanese martial arts that emphasize spiritual, social and civic qualities in their training. The kanji for *bu* (武) consists of two "radicals" which combine to mean "turning weapons;" *do* (道) is a spiritual path: a monk walks an endless road.

武
道

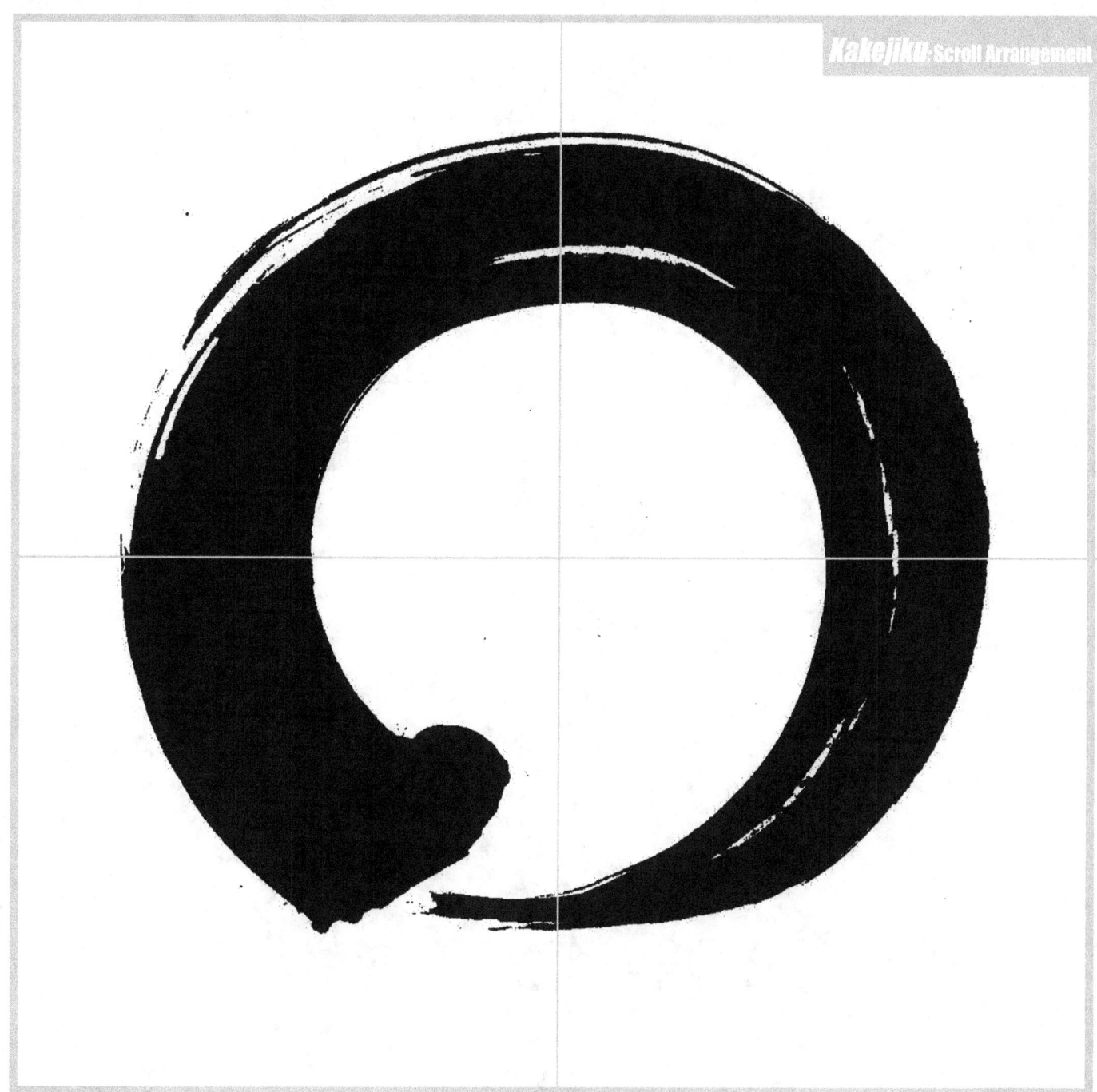

Shodo: *Brush Calligraphy*
Ensō (円相) - Circle

One of the most common calligraphic subjects in *Zen* (禅) Buddhism. A symbol, not a character, an *ensō* suggests the Absolute, enlightenment, strength, elegance, the Universe, and the indescribable Void; it also can symbolize Japanese aesthetics. Brushed "in the moment," *ensō* is an ancient Japanese version of minimalist, abstract expressionist art.

Enso by Yamada Mumon (1900-1988). The text reads:
"Nothing lacking, nothing in excess."

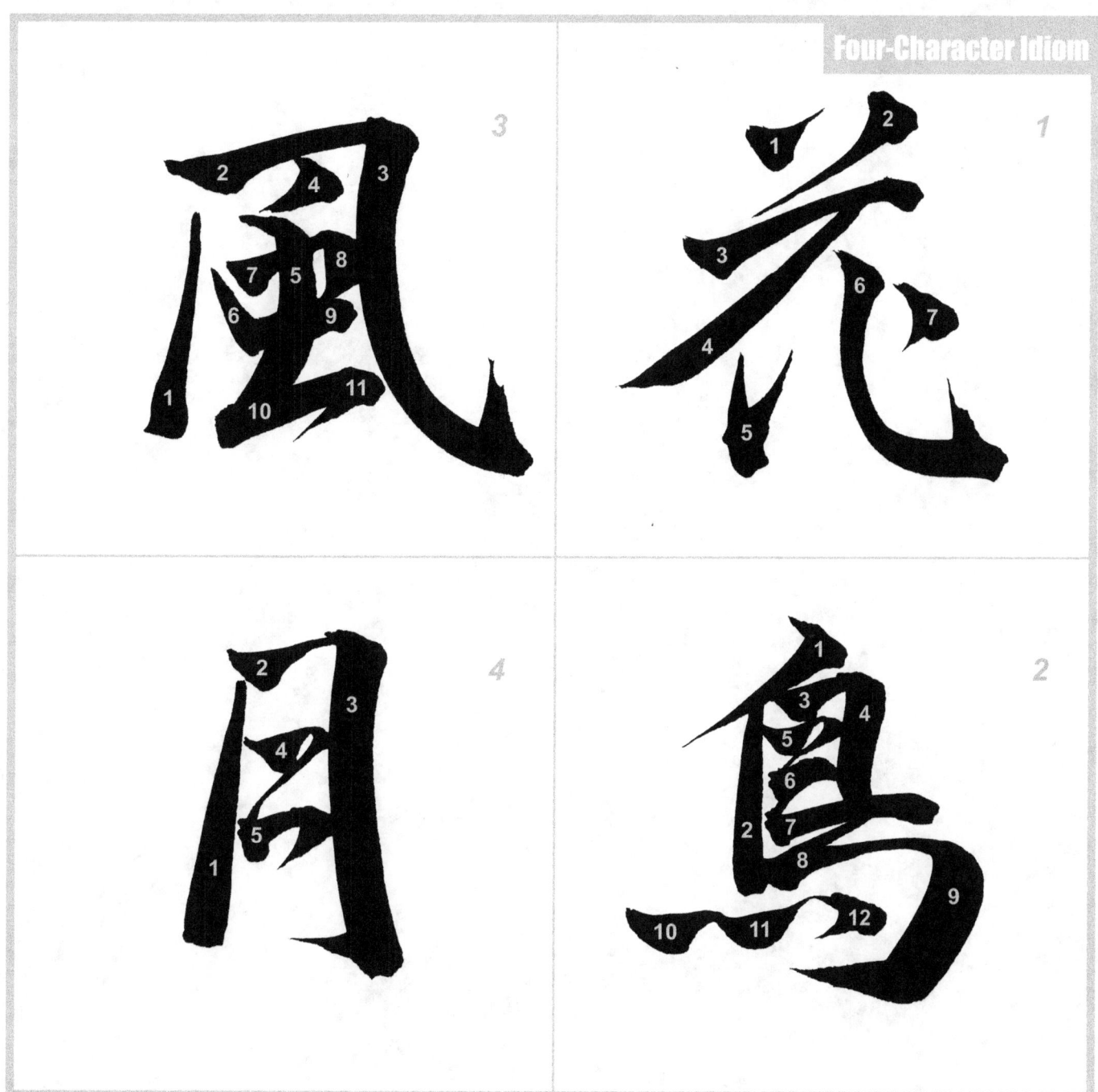

Shodo: *Brush Calligraphy*
Kaa-Fou-Chou-Getsu (花鳥風月) - The Beauties of Nature:
Flowers, Birds, Wind, Moon

A recurrent theme in Japanese literature: the importance of acknowledging seasonal change.

花
鳥
風
月

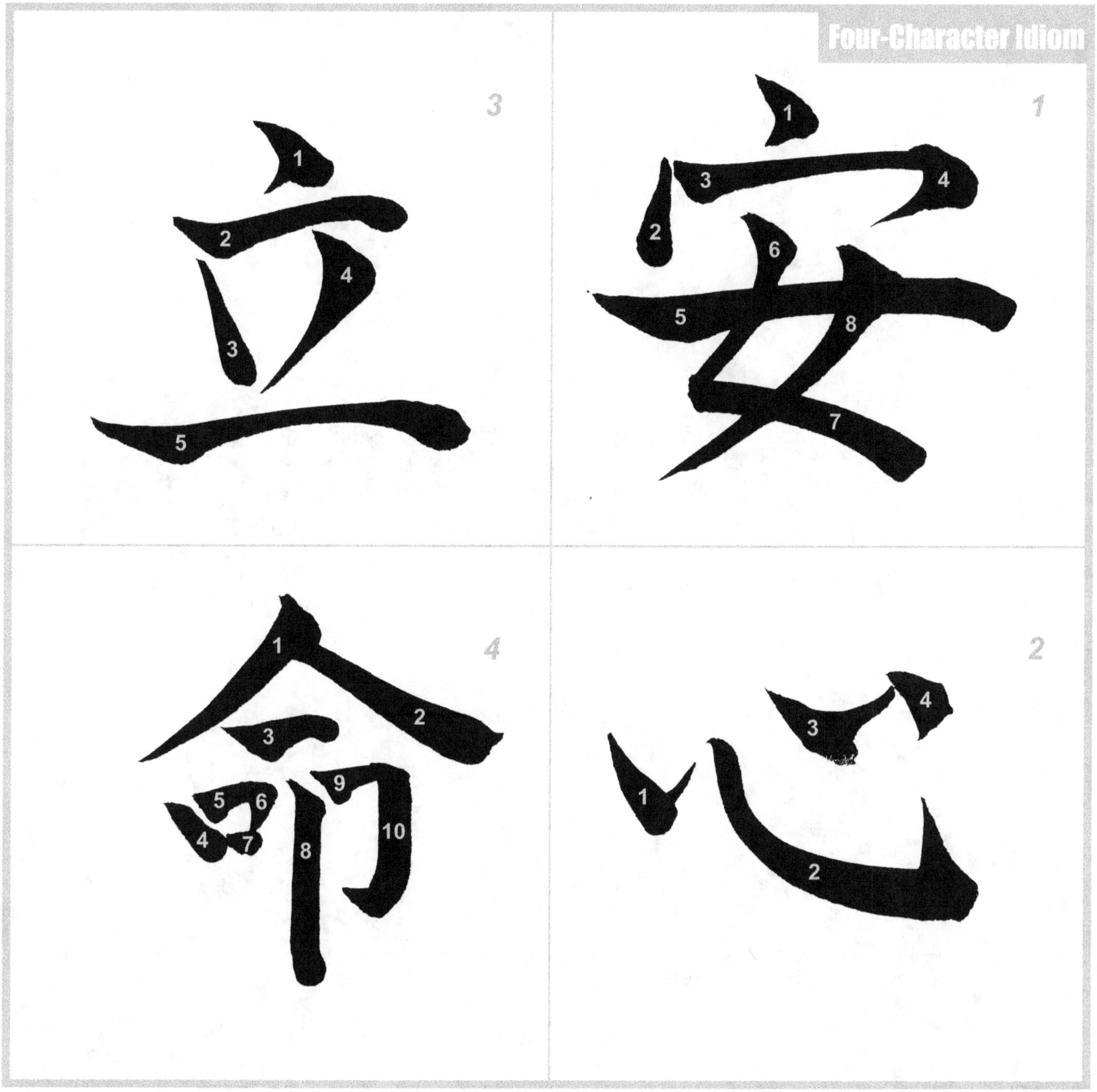

Shodo: *Brush Calligraphy*
An-Shin-Ritsu-Mei (安心立命) - Religious Enlightenment;
Spiritual Peace Achieved Through Faith

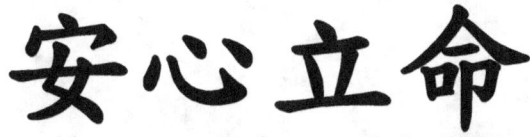

AnShin (安心) are two common kanji in Japanese advertising. They combine a concept of ease with the kanji for "heart," "mind," or "spirit" to indicate peace of mind. *Ritsu* (or *Tachi*) (立) is the kanji for "stand," but is used in compounds like "independence (自立)" or "national (国立)." Combined with *mei* (命), a kaniji meaning "life," "command," "spirit," or "decree," peace of mind is suggested again.

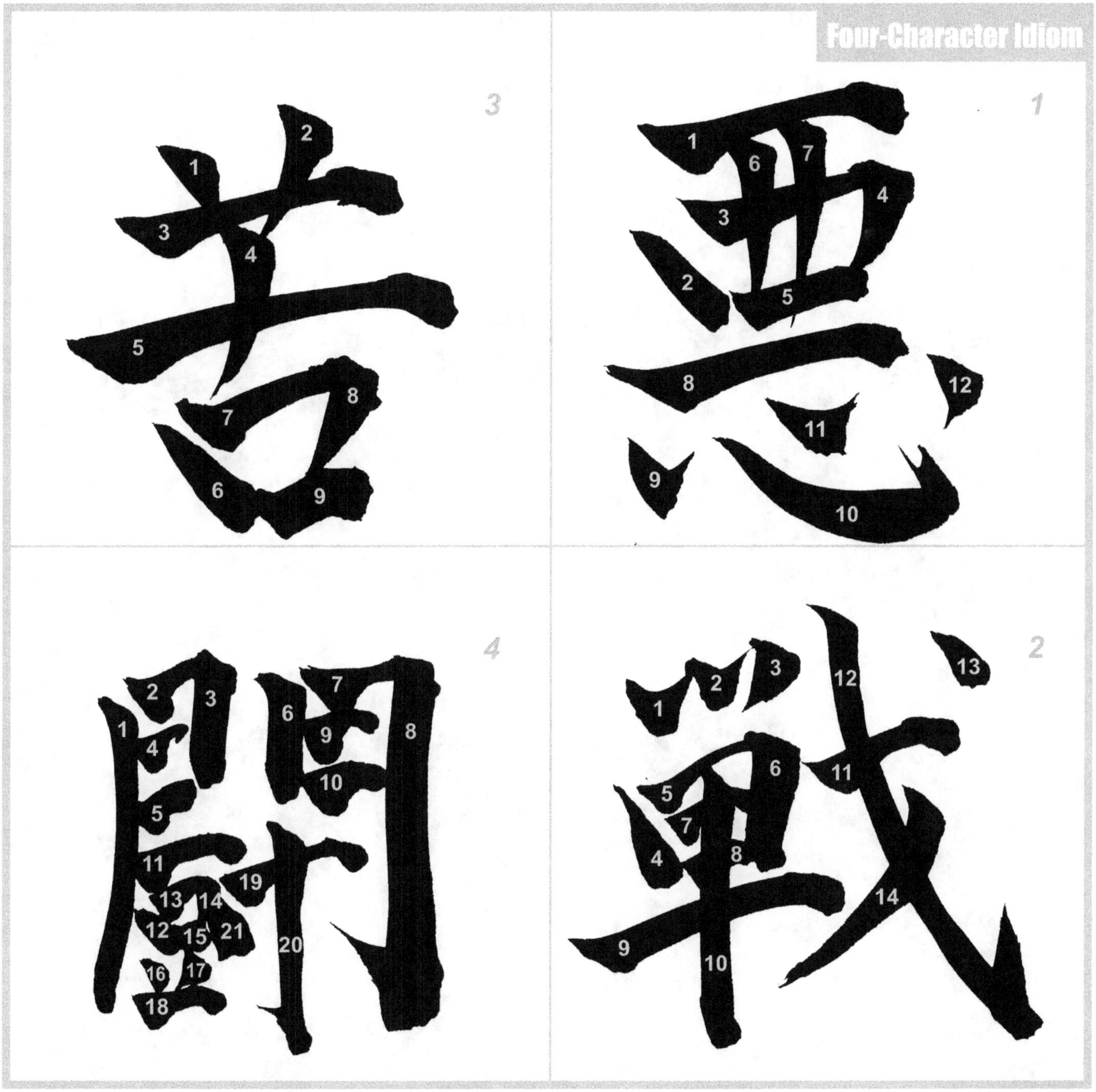

Shodo: *Four Character Ideom*
Aku-Sen-Ku-Tou (悪戦苦闘) - Struggle Hard Against Wrong-Doing (Evil)

Aku (悪) means "evil" or "vice;" *Sen* (戦) is "warfare;" *Ku* (苦) comes from *kurushii*, meaning "tough," "difficult," or "challenging;" *Tou* (闘) is "fight" or "battle."

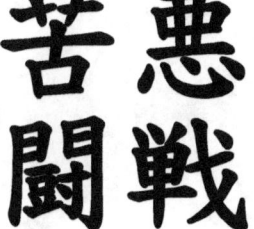

Shodo: *Brush Calligraphy*
Blank Worksheet

Good for Kids Too...

Numbers

10	9	8	7	6	5	4	3	2	1
十	九	八	七	六	五	四	三	二	一

Now you try!

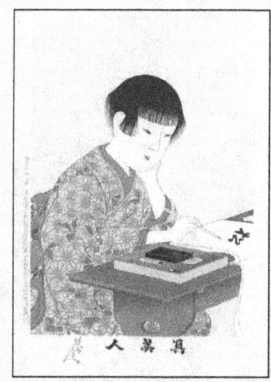
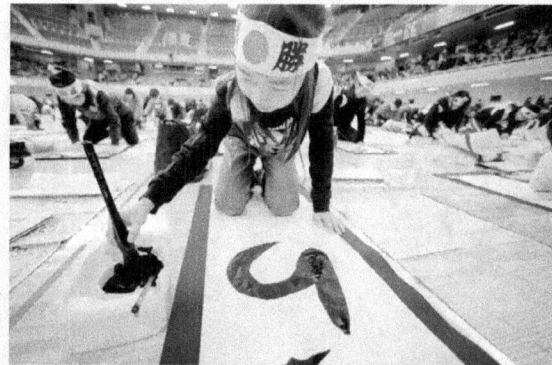
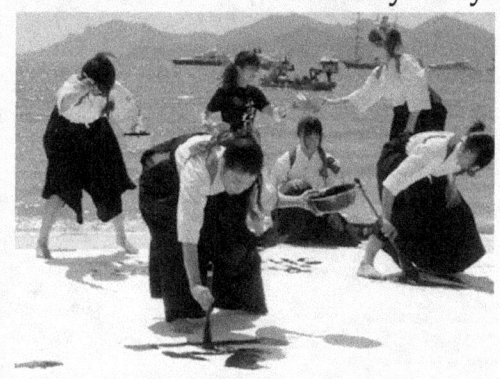

Let's write "Japan"

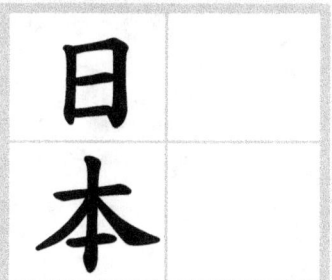

Sun (日)
Write them together to make "Nippon"

Land (本)
"Land of the Rising Sun"

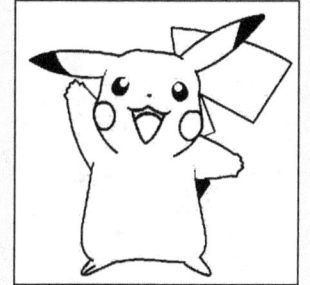

Can you brush *Pikachu*?

Part 3
Study Examples

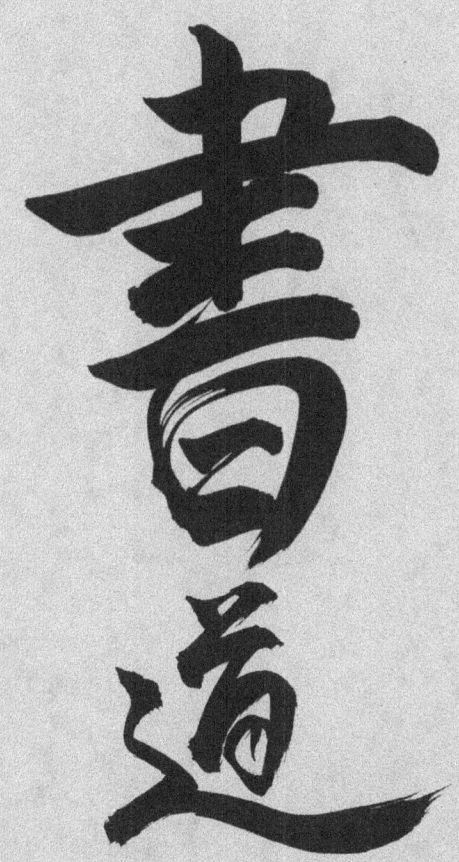

AiShinKai **Publications**
Self-Mastery in Daily Life
www.aishinkai.com

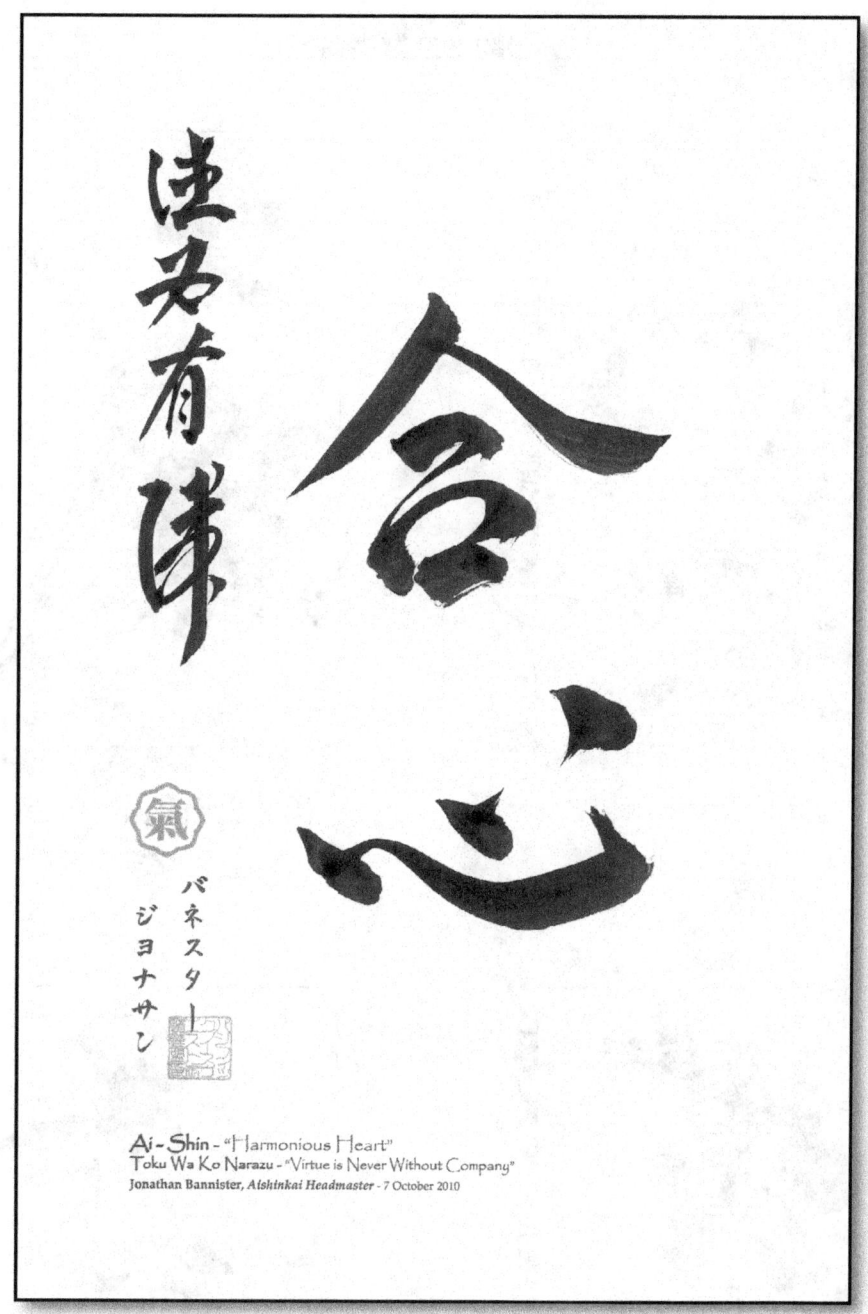

Shodo: *Brush Calligraphy Painting*
Ai-Shin (合心) - Harmonious Heart - *author calligraphy*

This rendition of the root name of our organization was brushed on the evening that our membership voted unanimous approval for a new name for our organization, **AiShinKai**. *AiShin* combines *Ai* (合) from Aikido with *Shin* (心), which can be variously interpreted as "God," "heart," "mind," "new," "truth," or "Center."

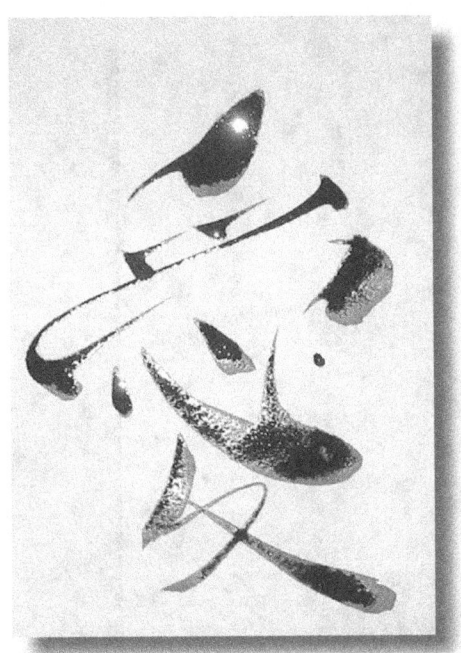

Ai - Love

愛

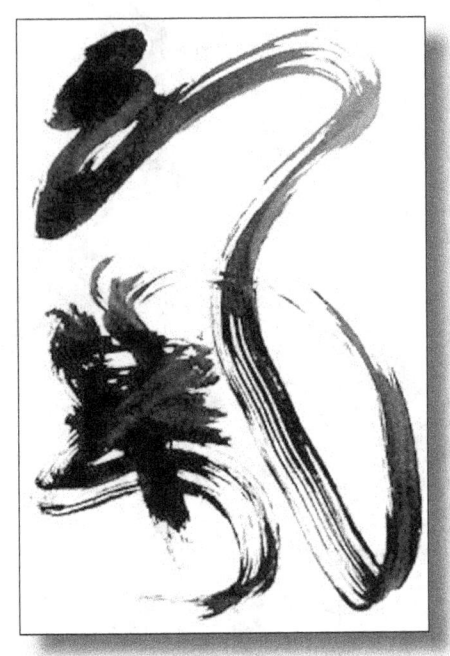

Ki - Spiritual Energy

氣

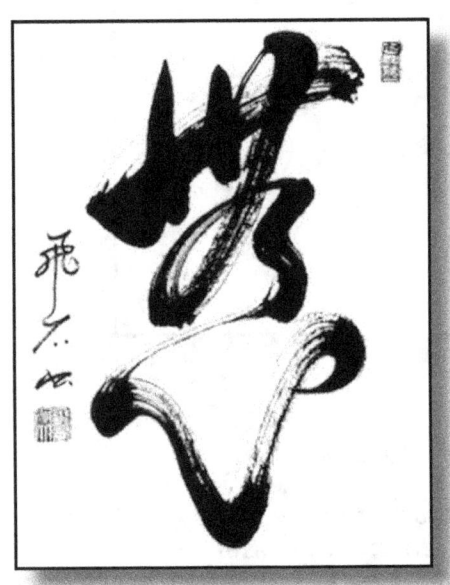

MuShin - No Mind

無心

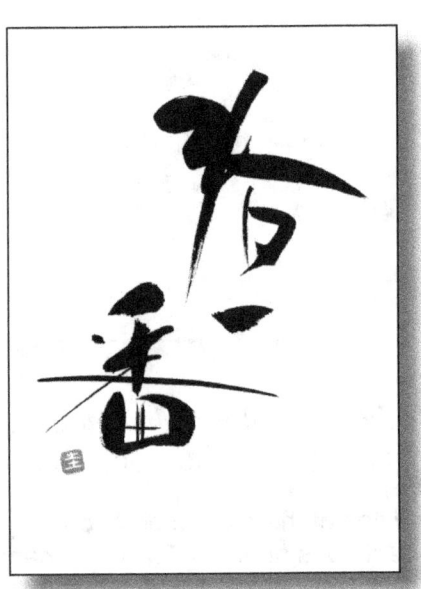

HaruIchiban - Spring is the Best

春一番

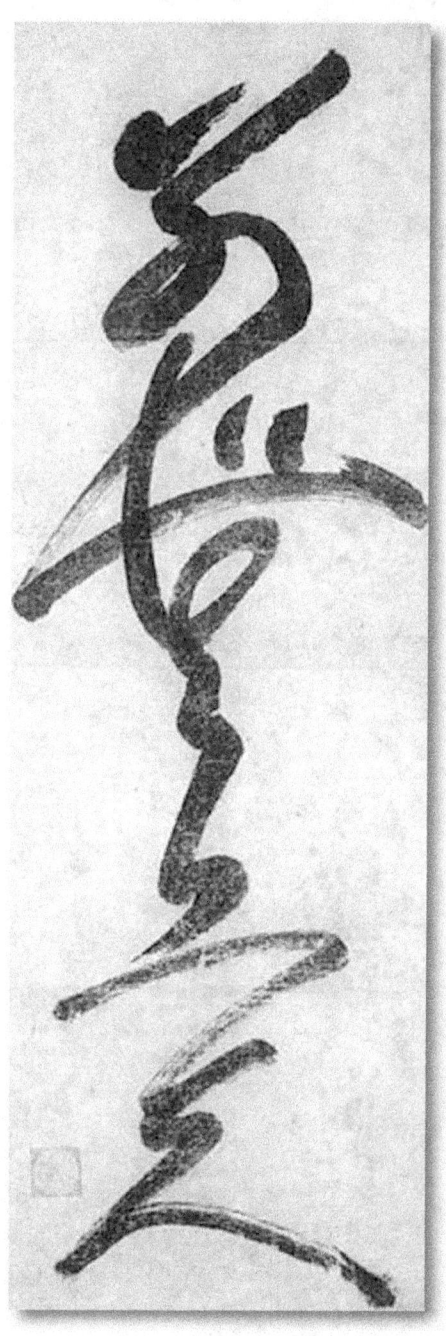
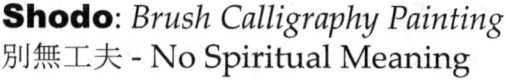

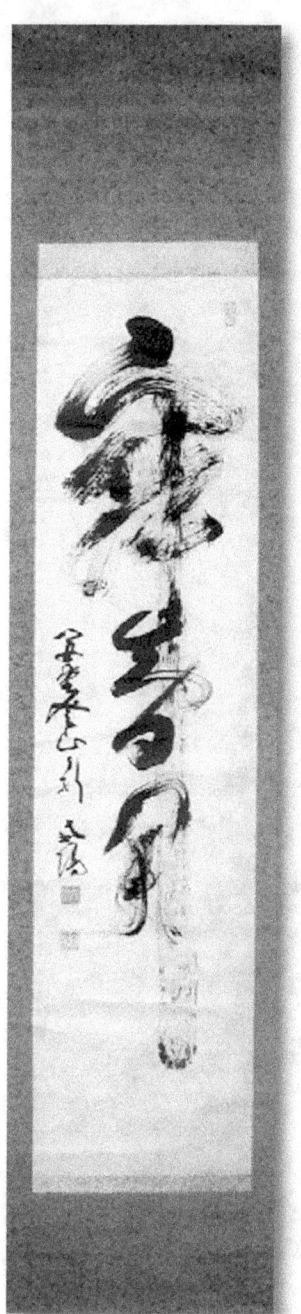

Shodo: *Brush Calligraphy Painting*
別無工夫 - No Spiritual Meaning

Musô Soseki (夢窓疎石), 1275 - 1351,
Zen master, poet, and garden designer.
His *sosho* style calligraphy is bold, free, and
well-composed. Firm horizontals anchor the
composition, and wonderful positive and
negative shapes create drama.

Shodo: *Brush Calligraphy Painting*
静恵劍 – Tranquil Wisdom Sword

Kasumi Bunsho (春見文勝), 1905-1998,
Zen master, a prolific and famous Shodo
artist. This dynamic composition features
an amazing vertical stroke through the
central kanji to make a sword.

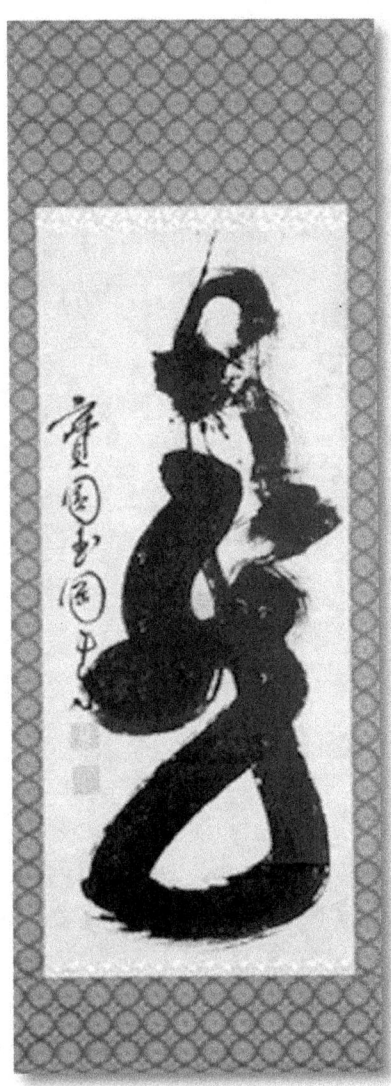

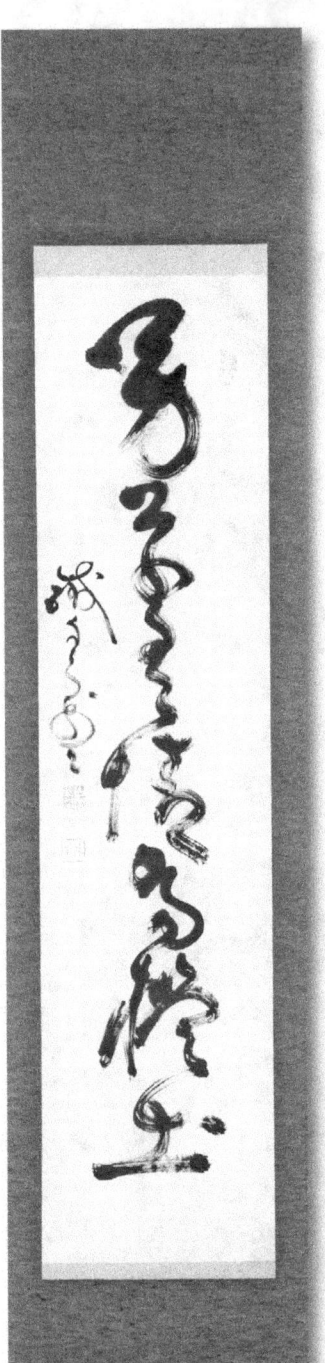

Shodo: *Brush Calligraphy Painting*
Ryuu (龍) - Dragon

Gyokko of Hoen[-*ji*, "Jade Hill" (1786-1881),
Soto Zen monk famed for talismatic dragon
paintings. The character writhes with
tremendous vitality. Compare this to *Shoko
Hirose*'s rendition of the same subject
on page 99.

Shodo: *One-Line Calligraphy Painting*
Fragrant Grass Has Passion

Tesshu Koho (*Tesshu Yamaoka*), 1836-1888,
One of the most famous and prolific *Zen*
samurai painters. The lively brush work
matches the theme. *Tesshu* was a famous
master of Japanese swordsmanship, a lay
Buddhist preacher, and advisor to the *Meiji*
emperor. He approached calligraphy with
the same ferocity as all other aspects of
his rich and inspiring life.

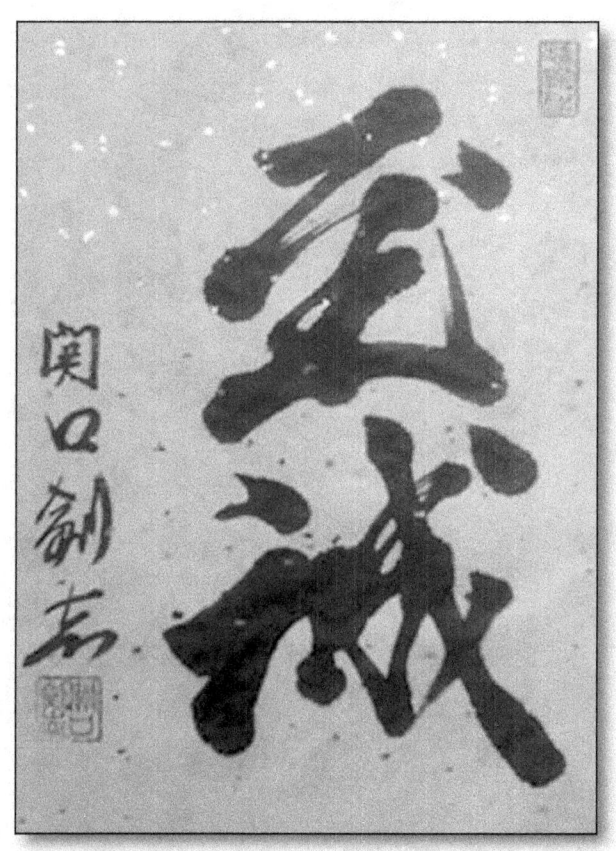

Shodo: *Brush Calligraphy Painting*
Shisei (至誠) - Sincerity

Powerful calligraphy by **Kenji Sekiguchi**
(関口剣志), noted calligrapher and swordsman.

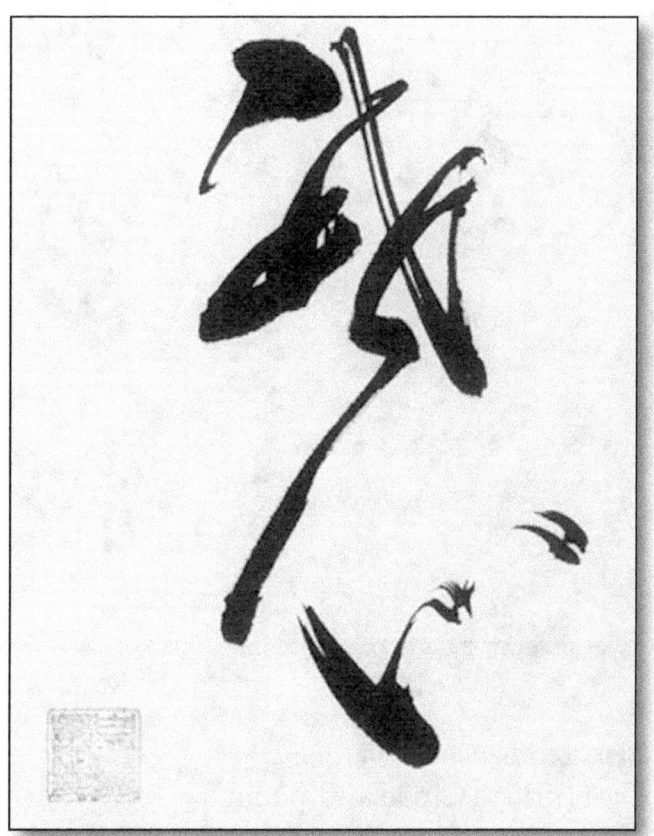

Shodo: *Brush Calligraphy Painting*
BuShin (武心) - Warrior Mind

Calligraphy by **Masaaki Hatsumi** (初見良昭),
born 1931, is *Soke*, or grandmaster of the
BujinKan, a famous martial arts school in Noda,
Chiba, Japan. This beautiful calligraphy in
sosho style elegantly captures the ephemeral
lightness of mind so desirable in the martial arts.

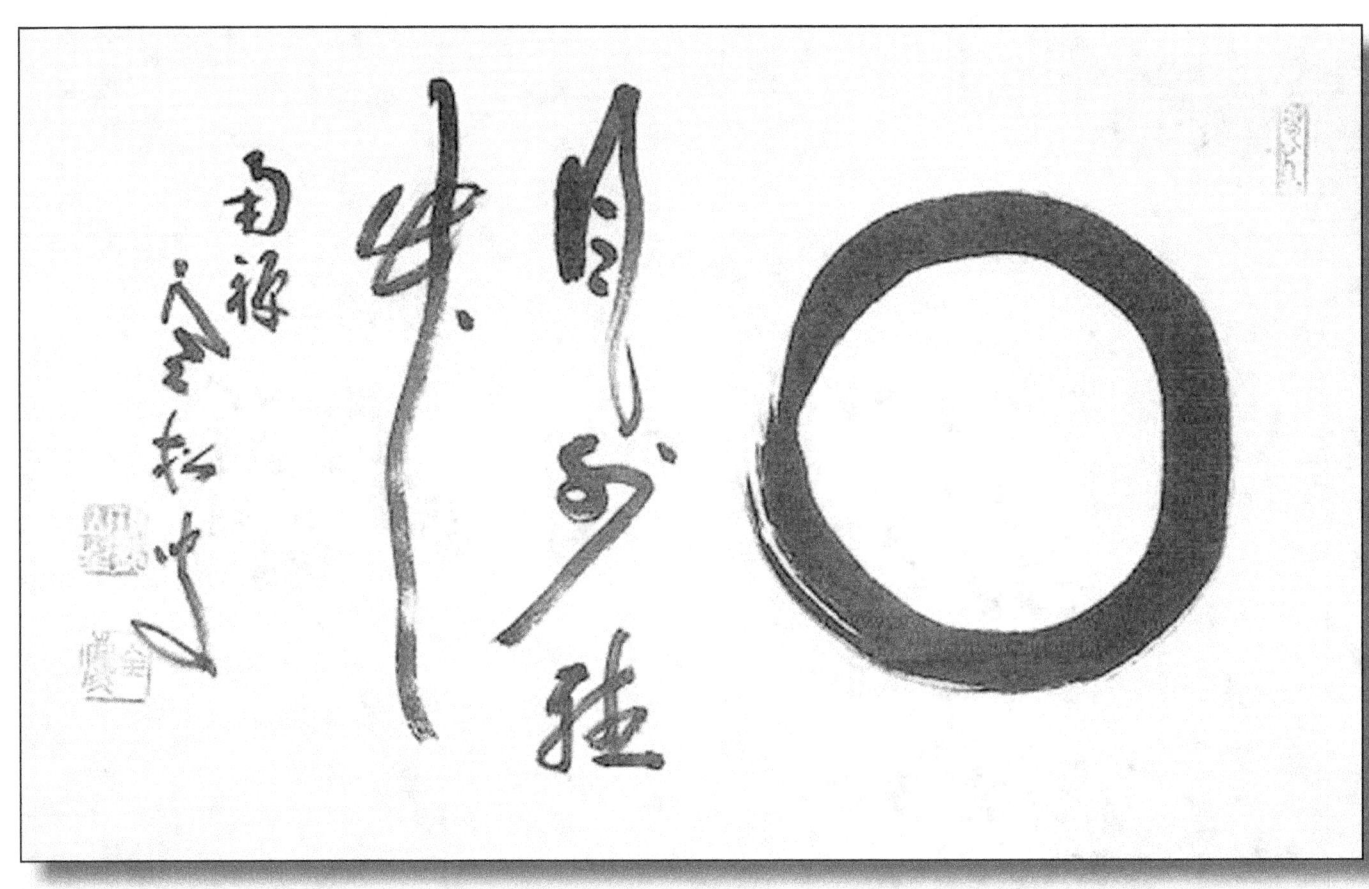

Shodo: *Brush Calligraphy*
Ensō (円相) - Circle and poem

Ensō and first line of a classical poem by **Shibayama Zenkei** (柴山全慶) (1894-1974), former abbot of *Nanzen-ji Zen* Buddhist temple in Kyoto, Japan. The calligraphy reads "Beyond the wind, listen to the bamboo," followed by his signature. The second line of text is a single kanji character stretched out, the character for "bamboo" (竹) , which Shibayama has altered to mimic the shape of a single, tall stalk.

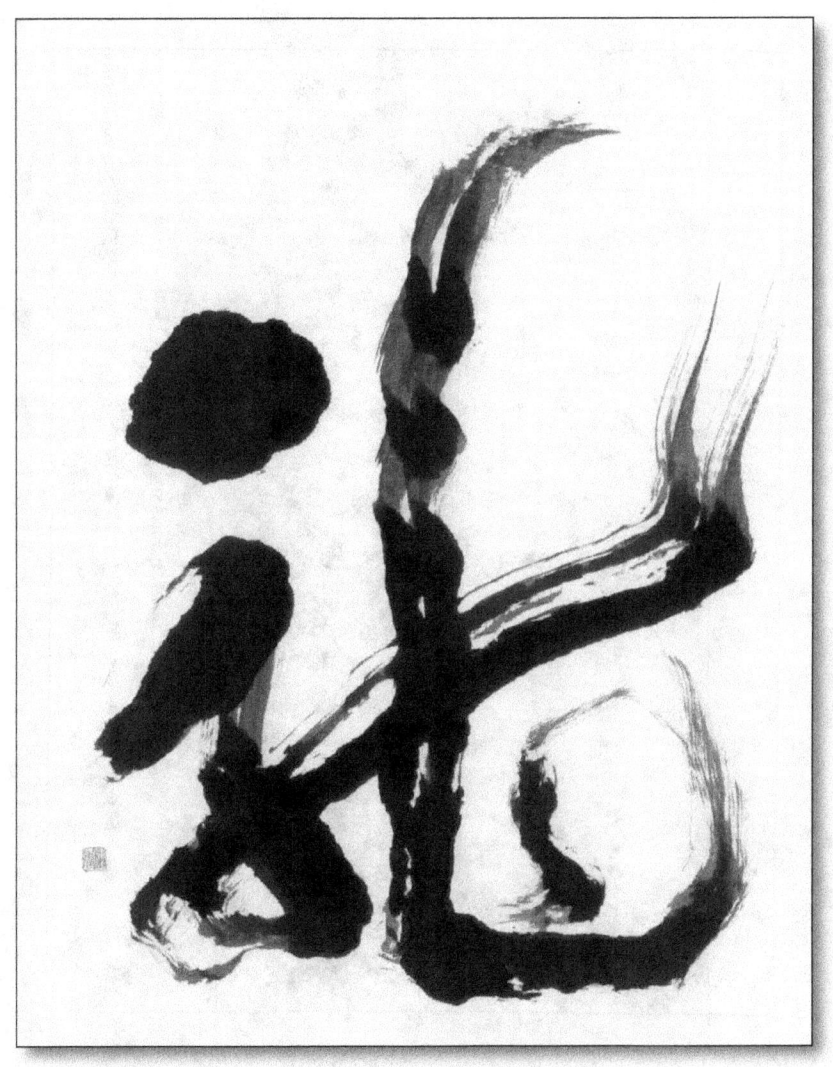

Shodo: *Brush Calligraphy Painting*
Ryu (龍) - Dragon

Calligraphy by **Shoko Hirose**, a modern master from Itikava, Japan.
This rendition explodes with sinuous energy. Can you sense the
vitality of the monster? Japan's dragons are wingless deities
associated with waterfalls and rain.

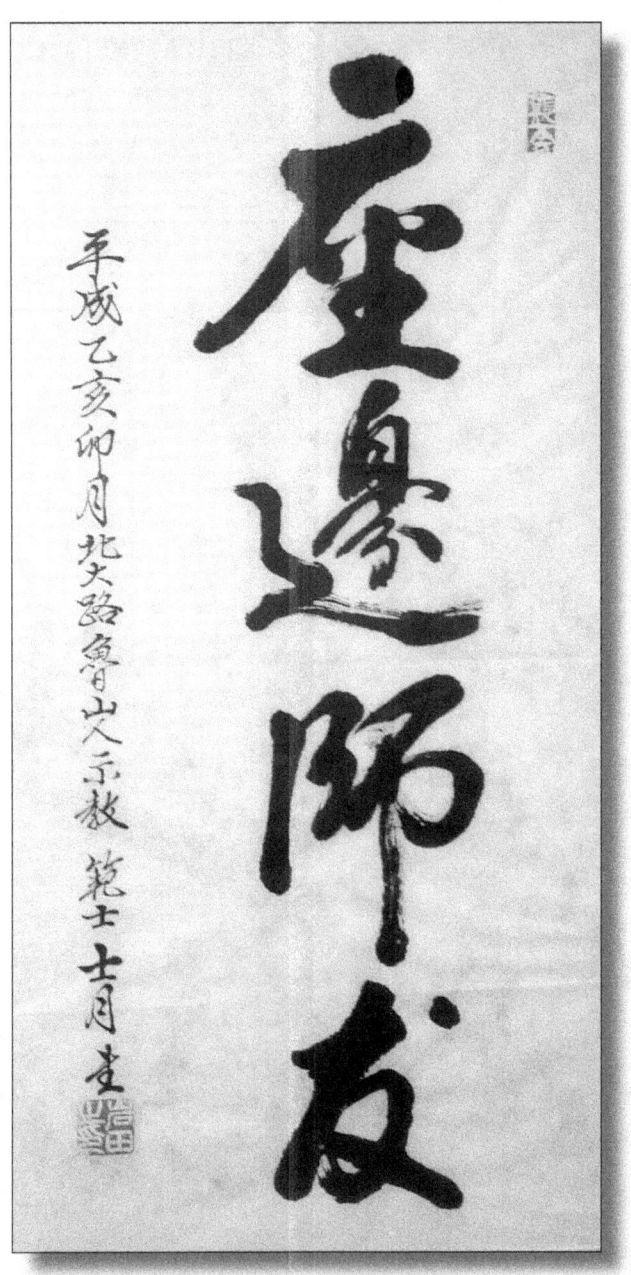

Shodo: *Brush Calligraphy Painting*
Zen Hen Shi Yu - 20th century

Calligraphy by the late ***Iwata Norikazu***, a modern master of brush and sword. It is a poem, translating "Sit beside your Teacher, learn from the past, surrounded by great works of art." This painting is in the collection of the ***AiShinKai***. It was presented by our organization by swordsman Ken Maneker of ShinKenKai dojo in Vancouver, British Columbia at the dedication of our new headquarters. The calligraphy is very fine, fluid and beautifully composed.

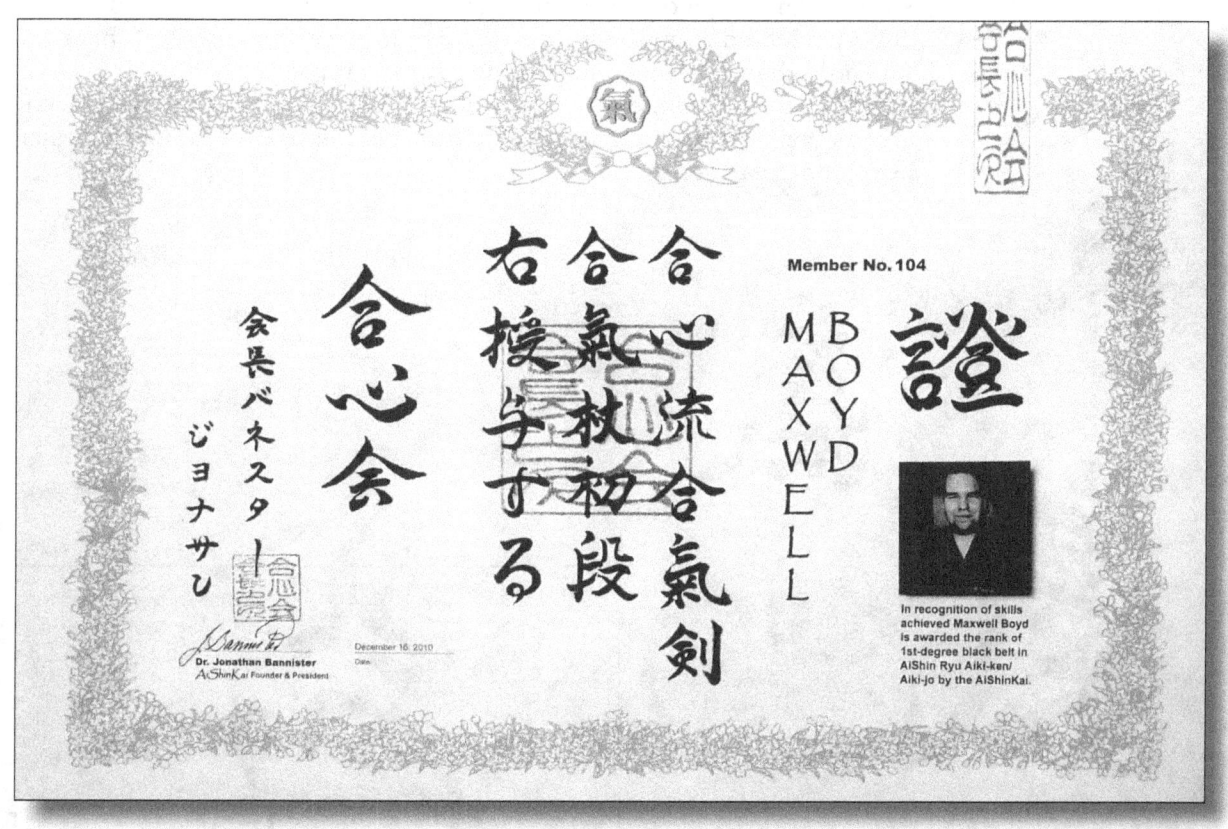

Shodo: *Brush Calligraphy Painting*
AiShinKai *Menjyo* 免許 (grade certificate) - 2010

Certification of first-degree black belt rank in *AiShin-Ryu Aiki-ken/Aiki-jo* presented in 2010 to AiShinKai member Mr. Maxwell Boyd. Black belt certificates are individually brushed by the author and are a source of great pride by our students. The border design, also hand-drawn by the author, is a modern rendition of a cherry blossom border used on Japanese, pre-war certificates of merit in swordsmanship. The final artwork, fixed with the official seals of the *AiShinKai*, is presented upon successful completion of a rigorous examination.

The composition and execution of such official documents is very difficult, and requires a great deal of time. It is a fitting token of respect for a student's hard work and accomplishment.

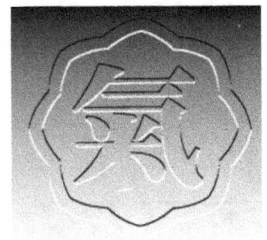

Evolution of a Character: *Ki* (氣)

My personal crest, or *mon*, is also the crest of the *AiShinKai*. It features a lotus flower surrounding the kanji for *Ki* (氣), or spiritual power, a very important symbol for practitioners of the martial art of Aikido. Representing a pot of rice boiling over fire, the impression is of a dynamic energy released from the inside. I have practiced this essential character for more than 30 years, and through the examples shown can trace the evolution of my understanding not just of Shodo, but of the martial arts as well. This is a great example of brushwork revealing the inner development of self-mastery.

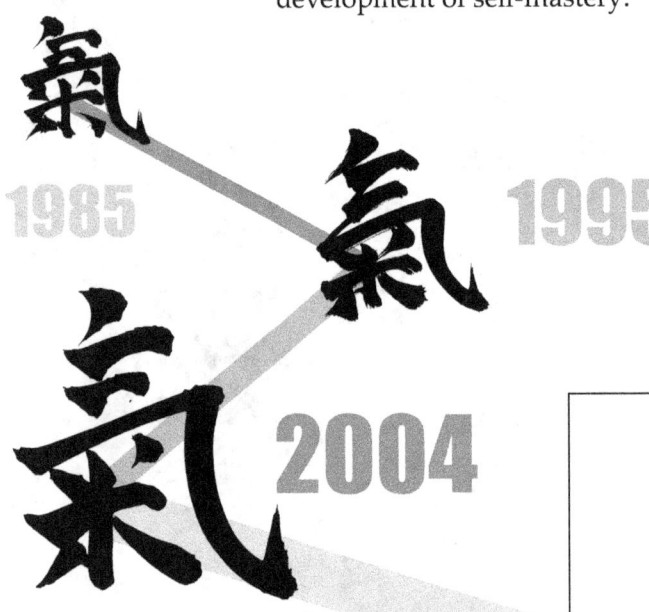

1985

1995

2004

2006

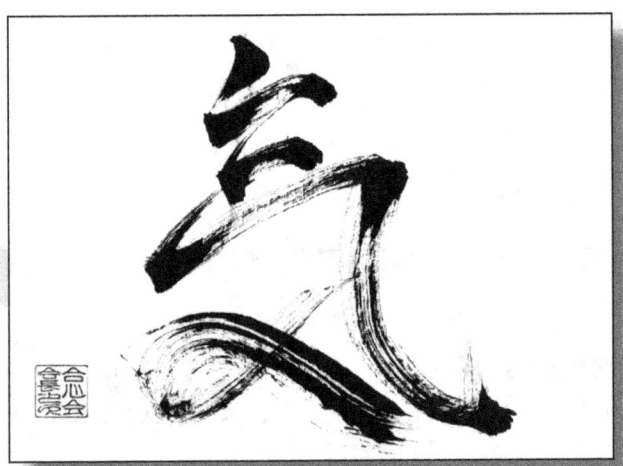

My early renditions of *Ki* lacked clarity, control and purpose. By 2004 I could manage well-developed compositions coupled with fairly precise brushwork. Then, in Spring 2006, I suddenly experienced a tremendous epiphany in martial arts practice. Techniques of the martial and cultural arts - even the management and negotiation skills I use in business - all became much more free and dynamic, with none of the tentativeness and stress that had marked earlier efforts. As a result, I can now exercise leadership, paint, perform, and teach with a profoundly relaxed body and mind, and with results more dynamic than ever before. This is the spirit of that lies at the heart of *AiShinKai* self-mastery training.

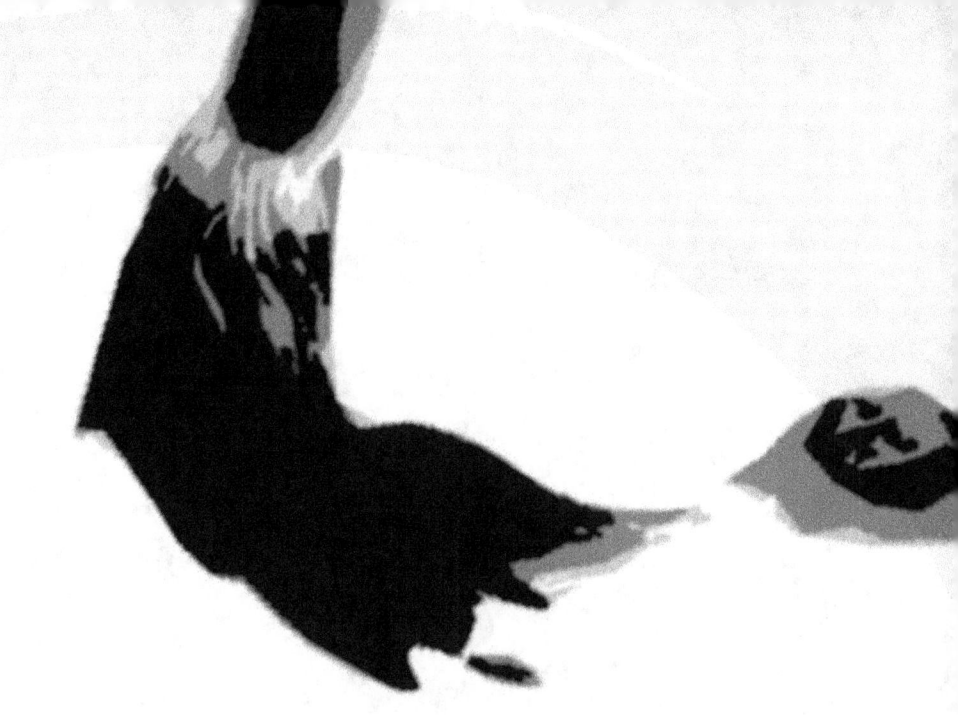

World Wide Web

AiShinKai LLC
http://www.aishinkai.com

JapanCalligraphy
http://www.japancalligraphy.eu/

Japan Guide
http://www.japan-guide.com/e/e2095.html

Kampo Cultural Center (web site) *Japanese Calligraphy*
http://www.kampo-bahal.com/about/JapaneseCalligraphy.htm

Kids Web Japan
http://web-japan.org/kidsweb/virtual/shodo/index.html

OnMarkProductions - *Calligraphy*
http://www.onmarkproductions.com/html/calligraphy1.shtml

Takase Shodokan
http://www.takase.com/LearnJapaneseCalligraphy/ShodoLessons/CD001/S001/L001/L001.htm

Wikipedia - *Japanese Calligraphy*
http://en.wikipedia.org/wiki/Japanese_calligraphy

Zen Shodo
http://www.zenshodo.com/history.htm

Books & Publications

Aria, Barbara with Russell Eng Gon, *The Spirit of the Chinese Character: Gifts from the Heart*. Chronicle Books, San Francisco, California, 1992.

Bannister, Dr. Jonathan, *The Path to Self-Mastery: Mind-Body Coordination Exercises from the Martial Arts to Achieve Peak Performance*. AiShinKai Publications, Edmonds, WA, 2011.

Frame, Susan, *Japanese Ink Painting: Beginner's Guide to Sumi-E*. Sterling Publishing Co., Inc., New York, New York, 2002.

Meito Shodokai: *Returning to One's True Self*. 10 Years Anniversary calligraphy exhibit catalog. Meito Japanese Calligraphy Association, Redmond, Washington, 2006.

Reed, William, *Shodo: The Art of Coordinating Mind, Body and Brush*. Japan Publications, 1990.

Rowley, Michael, *Kana Pict-O-Graphix: Mnemonics for Japanese Hiragana and Katakana*. Stone Bridge Press, Berkeley, California, 1995.

Ryokushu, Kuiseko, *Brush Writing: Calligraphy Techniques for Beginners*. Kodansha International, New York, 1988.

Shimano, Eido Tai, *Zen Word, Zen Calligraphy*. Shambhala, Boston, 1992.

Stevens, John, *The Sword of No Sword: Life of the Master Warrior Tesshu*. Shambhala Publications, Inc., Boston, Massachusetts, 1984.

Warner, Gordon and Donn F. Draeger, *Japanese Swordsmanship: Technique and Practice*. Weatherhill, New York, New York, 1984.

Museums

Seattle Asian Art Museum
1400 East Prospect Street
Seattle, WA 98112–3303
(206) 654-3100
www.seattleartmuseum.org

Wing Luke Museum
719 South King Street
Seattle, WA 98104
(206) 623-5124
www.wingluke.org

Asian Art Museum of San Francisco
200 Larkin Street
San Francisco, CA 94102
(415) 581-3500
www.asianart.org

Metropolitan Museum of Art
1000 Fifth Avenue
New York, NY 10028
(212) 535-7710
www.metmuseum.org

In Japan: Tokyo National Museum, Japan Calligraphy Museum, Taito Ward Calligraphy Museum.

Shodo Supplies

Most art supply stores will have some Shodo tools and materials

AiShinKai LLC
(425) 771-6816
www.aishinkai.com

University of Washington Book Store
4326 University Way NE
Seattle, WA 98105
(206) 634-3400
www.bookstore.washington.edu

Uwajimaya, Inc.
600 5th Avenue South
Seattle, WA 98104
(206) 624-6248

Daiso
710 6th Avenue
Seattle, WA 98104
(206) 623-5472

Daiso - Alderwood Mall
3000 184th Street SW Suite 398
Lynnwood, WA 98037
(425) 673-1825

The House of Rice Store
3221 N. Hayden Road
Scottsdale, AZ 85251
(480)947-6698
http://www.houserice.com/
    japsumpainse.html

Daniel Smith - Seattle
4150 First Avenue South
Seattle, Washington 98134

Oriental Art Supply
21522 Surveyor Circle
Huntington Beach, CA 92646
(714) 969-4470
www.orientalartsupply.com

Artistic Chinese Calligraphy
www.artisticchinesecalligraphy.com

Awesome Art Supply
www.awesomeartsupply.com

Kinokuniya Bookstores of America
525 South Weller St.
Seattle, WA 98104
(206) 587-2477

The Art of Calligraphy
Shodo artist Nadja Van Ghulue
Excellent advice concerning Shodo
supplies and equipment
http://www.theartofcalligraphy.com/
    japanese-calligraphy-supplies.html

Dick Blick Art Materials - Seattle
1600 Broadway Avenue
Seattle, WA 98122
(206) 324-0750
http://www.dickblick.com/

Shodo terminology is fairly consistent amongst calligraphers. For example, a brush is called *fude* without exception. However, the names of particular strokes are different in each school, and individual teachers will have different names for the same thing.

Romaji	Hiragana	Japanese	English
bunchin	ぶんちん	文鎮	Paperweight
dango	だんご	団子	Round Dumpling
fude	ふで	筆	Brush
fudejiku	ふでじく	筆軸	Brush Handle
fudemaki	ふでまき	筆巻	Brush Holder
fudeoki	ふでおき	筆置	Brush Rest
gampi	がんぴ	雁皮	gampi (washi material)
goumou fude	ごうもうふで	剛毛筆	Stiff Bristle Brush
hanshi	はんし	半紙	9 1/2" W x 13"H paper
juumou fude	じゅうもうふで	柔毛筆	Soft Bristle Brush
kami	かみ	紙	Paper
kasure	かすれ	掠れ	Texture made by brushwork openings
kengou fude	けんごうふで	兼豪筆	Mixed Hair Brush
keshou nori	けしょうのり	化粧糊	Weak glue to form brush tip
kofude	こふで	小筆	Kana Brush
kouzo	こうぞ	楮	kozo (washi material)
kyuujuuken	きゅうじゅうけん	歙州硯	Type of Suzuri
mitsumata	みつまた	三椏	mitsumata (washi material)
nachiguro	なちぐろ	那智黒	Type of Suzuri
nihon-ken	にほんけん	日本硯	Japanese Suzuri
nijimi	にじみ	滲み	Blotted area
riku	りく	陸	Land (grinding area of the ink stone)
ryuukeiken	りゅうけいけん	龍渓硯	Type of suzuri
shitajiki	したじき	下敷	Calligraphy Pad
suiteki	すいてき	水滴	Drop of Water
sumi	すみ	墨	Sumi (Indian) Ink
sumioki	すみおき	墨置	Sumi Rest
suzuri	すずり	硯	Ink Stone
tankei	たんけい	端渓	Area in China famous for Suzuri.
tankei-ken	たんけいけん	端渓硯	Suzuri from Tankei
umi	うみ	海	Ocean (well of the ink stone)
urauchi	うらうち	裏打ち	Backing art onto heavier paper
washi	わし	和紙	Japanese Paper (Washi)
yokoga	よこが	横画	Horizontal Line
youmou fude	ようもうふで	羊毛筆	Goat Hair Brush

Kanji List

Kanji characters can be fun to write, especially if you know what they mean. I have included this fairly exhaustive list because I have found it to be a great help in understanding the hidden meanings of the symbols. They are organized by family, so you may have to dig for a specific word. But once you find it, you'll be able to compare other uses of the character to glean a deeper appreciation of its content.

1.	人	Jin, Nin, hito	Human being, man, person
2.	一	Ichi, Itsu, hito(tsu), hito-	One
3.	二	Ni, futa(tsu), futa-	Two
4.	三	San, mit(tsu), mi(tsu), mi-	Three
5.	日	Nichi, Jitsu, hi, -ka	Day; sun
6.	四	Shi, yot(tsu), yo(tsu), yo-, yon	Four
7.	五	Go, itsu(tsu), itsu-	Five
8.	六	Roku, mut(tsu), mu(tsu), mu-, [mui]	Six
9.	七	Shichi, nana(tsu), nana, [nano-]	Seven
10.	八	Hachi, yat(tsu), ya(tsu), ya-, [yō]	Eight
11.	九	Kyuu, Ku, kokono(tsu), kokono-	Nine
12.	十	Juu, Ji', tō, to-	Ten
13.	円	En // maru(i)	Circle; yen // Round
14.	百	Hyaku	Hundred
15.	千	Sen, chi	Thousand
16.	万	Man / Ban	Ten Thousand / Many, all
17.	月	Getsu, tsuki / Gatsu	Moon; Month
18.	明	Mei	Light
		Myou	Light; next
		A(kari)	Light, Clearness
		Aka(rui)	Bright
		Aki(raka)	Clear
		A(keru) / Aka(rumu) / Aka(ramu)	Become light
		A(ku)	Be open
		A(kasu)	Pass (the night); Divulge
		A(kuru)	Next, following
	明日	Myounichi, Asu	Tomorrow
19.	曜	You	Day of the week
	曜日	youbi	Day of the week
20.	火	Ka, hi [ho]	Fire
	火曜日	Kayoubi	Tuesday
21.	水	Sui, mizu	Water
	水曜日	Suiyoubi	Wednesday
	水がめ	Mizugame	Water jug/jar
	水かさ	Mizukasa	Volume of water (of a river)
22.	木	Boku, Moku, ki [ka]	Tree; wood
	木曜日	Mokuyoubi	Thursday
	木こり	Kikori	Woodcutter, lumberjack, logger
	木	Kigi	Every tree; many trees
	千木	Chigi	Ornamental Crossbeams (on shrine)
	三木	Miki	(surname)
23.	金	Kin, Kon / Kane / [kana]	Gold, money, metal
	金曜日	Kinyoubi	Friday
	金ぱく	Kinpaku	Gold leaf/foil
	金もうけ	Kanemouke	Making money
24.	土	Do, To, tsuchi	Earth, soil, ground
	土曜日	Doyoubi	Saturday
	土人	Dojin	Native, Aborigine
	土のう	Donou	Sandbag
25.	本	Hon / moto	Book; origin; main; this; (counter for long, thin objects) / origin

	日本（人）	Nihon, Nippon (jin)	Japan (Japanese)
	本日	Honjitsu	Today
	本人	Honnin	The said person, the person himself
26.	大	Dai, Tai, ō(kii)	Big, large
		Ō(i ni)	Very much, greatly
	大金	Taikin	Large amount of money
	大きさ	ōkisa	Size
	大水	ōmizu	Flooding, overflow
	大みそか	ōmisoka	New Year's Eve
	大人	Otona	Adult
27.	小	Shō, chii(sai), ko-, o-	Little, small
	小人	Kobito	Dwarf, midget
		Shōjin	Insignificant person, small-minded man
		Shōnin	Child
	大小	Daishō	Large and small; size
	小金	Kogane	Small sum of money; small fortune
28.	中	Chuu / Naka	Middle; inside; throughout
	一日中	Ichinichichuu	All day long
	日中	Nitchuu	During the day
29.	風	Fuu [Fu] / Kaze [kaza]	Wind; appearance, style / wind
	日本風	Nihon-fuu	Japanese Style
	風土	Fuudo	Natural features, climate
	中風	Chūbū, chūfū	Paralysis, palsy
	そよ風	Soyokaze	Gentle breeze
30.	雨	U, ame [ama]	Rain
	風雨	Fūu	Wind and rain
	大雨	Ooame	Heavy Rain
	小雨	Kosame	Light Rain
	雨水	Amemizu	Rain water
	にわか雨	Niwaka ame	Sudden shower
31.	下	Ka, GE, shita, moto	Lower, base
		Shimo	Lower part
	下げる・下ろす・下す	Sa(geru) / o(rosu) / kuda(su)	Lower; hand down (verdict)
	下がる	Sa(garu)	Hang down, fall
	下りる	O(riru)	Get out of, get off (vehicle)
	下る	Kuda(ru)	Go / Come down
	下さる	Kuda(saru)	Give
	下水	Gesui	Sewer system, drainage
	風下	Kazashimo	Leeward side
32.	上	Jō, [Shō], ue	Upper
		Kami, [uwa-]	Upper part
	上げる	Ageru	Raise
	上がる・上る	A(garu) / Nobo(ru)	Rise
	上せる・上す	Nobo(seru) / Nobo(su)	Bring up (topic)
	水上	Suijō	On the water
	上下	Jōge	High and low, rise and fall
	上り下り	Nobori kudari	Ascent and Descent, ups and downs
33.	川	Sen, kawa	River
	川上	Kawakami	Upstream
	川下	Kawashimo	Downstream
	小川	Ogawa	Creek, brook, stream
	中川	Nakagawa	(surname)
34.	山	San, yama	Mountain
	山水	Sansui	Landscape, natural scenery
	火山	Kazan	Volcano
	下山	Gezan	Descent from mountain
	小山	Koyama	Hill
35.	田	Den, ta	Rice field, paddy
	水田	Suiden	Rice paddy
	田中・本田・山田	Tanaka / Honda / Yamada	(surname)

36.	畑	Hata, hatake	Cultivated field
	田畑	Tahata	Fields
37.	刀	Tō, katana	Sword
	日本刀	Nihontō	Japanese sword
	大刀	Daitō	Long sword
	小刀	Shōtō, kogatana	Short sword, knife, pocket knife
	山刀	Yamagatana	Woodsman's hatchet
38.	分	Bun, Bu	Portion, 1 percent
		Fun	Minute
	分ける・分かつ	Wa(keru) / Wa(katsu)	Divide, share, distinguish
	分かれる	Wa(kareru)	Be separated
	分かる	Wa(karu)	Understand
	十分	Jubun	Enough, sufficient, adequate
39.	切	Setsu, [Sai]	Cut
	切る	Ki(ru)	Cut
	切れる	Ki(reru)	cut well; break off; run out of
	大切	Taisetsu	Important, precious
	一切れ	Hitokire	Slice, piece
	切り上げ	Kiriage	Conclusion; rounding up; revaluation
	切り下げ	Kirisage	Reduction; Devaluation
40.	国	Koku, kuni	Country
	大国	Taikoku	Large / Great country
	万国	Bankoku	All Countries, world
41.	寺	Ji, tera	Temple
42.	時	Ji, toki	Time; hour
	時々	Tokidoki	Sometimes
	日時	Nichiji	Time, date, day and hour
43.	間	Kan, ken, aida / ma	Interval, between / interval; a room
	時間	Jikan	Time, hour
	中間	Chuukan	Middle, intermediate
	人間	Ningen	Human being
	間もなく	Mamonaku	Soon, before long, in a little while
44.	生	Sei, Shō	Life
	生きる・生ける	I(kiru/keru)	Be alive
	生かす	I(kasu)	Revive, bring to life; let live
	生む	U(mu)	Bear (a child)
	生まれる	U(mareru)	Be born
	生やす・生える	Ha(yasu/eru)	Grow
	生	Nama / ki-	Raw, draft (beer) / pure
45.	年	Nen, toshi	Year
	生年月日	Seinengappi	Date of birth
	（三）年生	(San)Nensei	(Third) Year student
	（五）年間	(Go)間	For (5) years
	年金	Nenkin	Pension, annuity
46.	以	I	(prefix)
	以上	Ijō	Or more; more than; above-mentioned
	以下	Ika	Or less; less than; as follows
47.	前	Zen, mae	Before, in front of, earlier
	以前	Izen	Ago, previously, formerly
	前もって	Maemotte	Before hand, in advance
	人前で	Hito mae de	In front of people
	分け前	Wakemae	One's share
	二人前	Nininmae, Futarimae	Enough for two people
48.	後	Go, nochi	After, later
	後ろ	Kō, ushi(ro)	Behind
	後	ato	Afterward, subsequent, back, retro-
	後れる	Oku(reru)	Be late, lag behind
	以後	Igo	Hereafter; since then
	前後	Zengo	Approximately; front and rear

110

	明後日	Myōgonichi / Asatte	Day after tomorrow
	その後	Sono ato	Thereafter, later
49.	午	Go	Noon
	午前	Gozen	Morning; a.m.
	午後	Gogo	Afternoon; p.m.
50.	先	Sen, saki	Earlier; priority; future; destination; the tip
	先日	Senjitsu	The other day, recently
	先月	Sengetsu	Last month
	先生	Sensei	Teacher
51.	今	Kon, Kin, ima	Now
	今日	Kyou, Konnichi	Today
	今月	Kongetsu	This month
	今年	Kotoshi	This year
	今後	Kongo	After this, from now on
	今ごろ	Imagoro	About this time (of day)
52.	入（る）	Nyū, hai(ru), i(ru)	Go / come / get in, enter
		i(reru)	Put / let in
	入国	Nyūkoku	Entering a country
	金入れ	Kaneire	Coin purse / wallet
	日の入り	Hi no iri	Sunset
	入日	Irihi	Setting Sun
53.	出（す）	Shutsu, [Sui], da(su)	Take out; send
	出る	Deru	Go / come out
	出火	Shukka	Outbreak of fire
	出入り	Deiri	Coming and going (of people)
	人出	Hitode	Turnout, crowd
	日の出	Hi no de	Sunrise
54.	口	Kō, Ku, kuchi	Mouth
	人口	Jinkō	Population
	入口	Iriguchi	Entrance
	出口	Deguchi	Exit
	川口	Kawaguchi	Mouth of a river
	口出し	Kuchidashi	Meddling, butting in
55.	目	Moku, [Boku], me, [ma]	Eye / (suffix for ordinals)
	一目	Hitome / ichimoku	A glance
	人目	Hitome	Notice, public attention
	目上	Meue	One's superior / senior
	目下	Meshita / mokka	One's subordinate / junior / at present
56.	耳	Ji, mimi	Ear
	耳目	Jimoku	Eye and ear; attention
	中耳	Chuuji	Middle ear
57.	手	Shu, te, [ta]	Hand
	切手	Kitte	Stamp
	小切手	Kogitte	Check ($)
	上手	Jouzu	Skilled
	下手	Heta	Unskilled
58.	足	Soku, ashi	Leg, foot
	足る・足りる	Ta(ru) / Ta(riru)	Be enough, sufficient
	足す	Ta(su)	Add up, add to
	一足	Issoku	One pair (shoe, socks, etc)
	手足	Teashi	Limbs, hands and feet
	足下に	Ashimoto ni	At one's feet, watch your step
59.	身	Shin, mi	Body
	身上	Shinjou	Strong point merit; personal background
		Shinshou	One's fortune, property
	出身	Shusshin	(be) From
	前身	Zenshin	Past life, predecessor
	身分	Mibun	Social standing, identity
60.	休（む）（める）（まる）	Kyuu, yasu(mu)(meru)(maru)	Rest / give it a rest / be rested

	休日	Kyūjitsu	Holiday, day off
	一休み	Hitoyasumi	Short rest
	休み中	Yasumichū	Closed (shop)
	休火山	Kyūkazan	Dormant volcano
61.	体	Tai, Tei, karada	Body
	身体	Shintai	Body
	人体	Jintai	Human body
	五体	Gotai	Whole Body
	大体	Daitai	Gist; on the whole; generally
	風体	Fūtai, Fūtei	Outward appearance
62.	自（ら）	Ji, Shi, mizuka(ra)	Self
	自分	Jibun	Oneself, one's own
	自身	Jishin	Oneself, itself
	自体	Jitai	One's own body
	自国	Jikoku	One's own country
	自らの手で	Mizukara no te de	With one's own hands
63.	見（る）	Ken, mi(ru)	See
	見える	Mi(eru)	Be visible
	見せる	Mi(seru)	Show
	一見	Ikken	Quick glance
	先見	Senken	Foresight
	見本	Mihon	Sample (of merchandise)
	見出し	Midashi	Headline, Heading
	見分ける	Miwakeru	Tell apart, recognize
64.	聞（く）（こえる）	Bun, Mon, Ki(ku)(koeru)	Hear, listen / be audible
	見聞	Kenbun	Information, observation, experience
	風聞	Fūbun	Hearsay, rumor
	聞き手	Kikite	Listener
	聞き入れる	Kiki ireru	Acede to, comply with
65.	取（る）	Shu, to(ru)	Take
	取り出す	Toridasu	Take out, pick out
	足取り	Ashidori	Way of walking, gait
	聞き取る	Kikitoru	Follow / catch what someone says
	日取り	Hidori	Appointed day
	取り上げる	Toriageru	Take up, adopt
66.	言	Gen, Gon, -koto	Word
	言（う）	I(u)	Say
	一言	Ichigoto, hitokoto	One word, a brief comment
	一言二言	Ichikoto futakoto	A word or two
	言明	Genmei	Definative statement, declaration
	小言	Kogoto	Scolding, complains, griping
	言い分	Iibun	One's say; objection
67.	語（る）	Go, kata(ru)	Talk, relate
	語（らう）	Katarau	Converse
	国語	Kokugo	National language
	言語	Gengo	Language, speech
	一語一語	Ichigo-ichigo	Word for word, verbatim
	語り手	Katarite	Narrator, storyteller
68.	行（く）	Kō, [An], i(ku),yu(ku)	Go
		Gyō	Line of text
	行（う）	Okonau	Do, perform, carry out
	一行	Ikkou	Party, retinue
	一行	Ichigyō	a line of text
	行間	Gyōkan	Space between line of text
69.	来（る）	Rai, ku(ru),kita(ru)	Come
	来（す）	Kita(su)	Bring about, cause
	来年	Rainen	Next year
	来月	Raigetsu	Next month
	来日	Rainichi	Come to Japan
	本来	Honrai	Originally, Primarily

	以来	Irai	Ever (since)
70.	方	Hō	Direction; side
		Kata	Person; method; side
	一方	Ippō	One side; on the other hand; only
	四方	Shihō	NSEW, All directions
	八方	Happō	All directions, all sides
	方言	Hōgen	Dialect
	目方	Mekata	Weight
71.	東	Tō, higashi	East
	東方	Tōhō	Eastward
	中東	Chūtō	Middle East
	東大	Tōdai	Tokyo University
72.	西	Sei, Sai, Nishi	West
	西方	Seihō	Westward
	東西	Tōzai	East and West
	西風	Seifū, Nishikaze	West wind
	西日	Nishibi	Afternoon sun
73.	北	Hoku, kita	North
	北方	Hoppō	Northward
	東北	Tōhoku	Region in northern Honshū
	北東	Hokutō	Northeast
74.	南	Nan, [Na], minami	South
	西南	Seinan	Southwest
	東南	Tōnan	Southeast
	南北	Nanboku	North and South
75.	左	Sa, hidari	Left
	左方	Sahō	Left side
	左手	Hidarite	Left hand
	左足	Hidariashi	Left leg / foot
	左目	Hidarime	Left eye
	左上	Hidariue	Upper left
76.	右	U, Yū, migi	Right
	右方	Uhō	Right side
	左右	Sayū	Left and right; control
	右手	Migite	Right hand
	右と言えば左	Migi to ieba hidari	(Always) arguing
77.	当（てる）（たる）	Tō, a(teru), a(taru)	Hit, be on target
	本当	Hontō	Truth; really
	当時	Tōji	At present; at that time
	当分	Tōbun	For now, for a while
	手当て	Teate	Allowance, compensation
			Medical treatment
78.	石	Seki, [Shaku], ishi	Stone
		[Koku]	Unit of volume about 180 liters
	石けん	Sekken	Soap
	木石	Bokuseki	Trees and stones, inanimate objects
	小石	Koishi	Pebbles, small stones
	石切	Ishikiri	Stone cutting, quarrying
79.	物	Butsu, Motsu, mono	Object, thing
	人物	Jinbutsu	Person, personage
	生物	Seibutsu	Living beings, life
	見物	Kenbutsu	Sightseeing
	物語	Monogatari	Tale, story
	本物	Honmono	Genuine, the real thing
80.	事	Ji, [ZU], koto	Thing
	人事	Jinji	Human / Personal affairs
	火事	Kaji	Fire
	事前	Jizen	Before the fact
	事後	Gozen	After the fact
	大事	Daiji	Great thing, important

	出来事	Dekigoto	Event, occurrence
81.	夕	Seki, yū	Evening
	一夕	Isseki	One evening
	夕方	Yūgata	Evening
	夕日	Yūhi	Evening / Setting sun
	夕月	Yūzuki	Evening moon
	七夕	Tanabata	Star Festival
82.	名	Mei, Myō, na	Name; reputation
	人名	Jinmei	Name of person
	名人	Meijin	Master, Expert, Virtuoso, Genius
	名物	Meibutsu	Noted product (of a locality)
	大名	Daimyō	Japanese feudal lord
	名前	Namae	Name
83.	外	Gai, Ge, soto	Outside
	外(れる/す)	Hazu(reru/su)	Slip off; remove; miss
	外国人	Gaikokujin	Foreigner
	外来語	Gairaigo	Word of foreign origin, loanword
	外出	Gaishutsu	Go out
	以外	Igai	Besides, except for
84.	内	Nai, [Dai], uchi	Inside
	国内	Kokunai	Domestic, internal
	体内	Tainai	Inside the body
	内外	Naigai	Inner and outer, domestic and foreign
	以内に	Inaini	Within
85.	死(ぬ)	Shin, shi(nu)	Death, die
	死体	Shitai	Dead body, corpse
	死人	Shinin	Dead person, the dead
	死後	Shigo	After death
	水死	Suishi	Drowning
	死語	Shigo	Dead language
86.	部	Bu	Part, section; copy of a publication
	一部	Ichibu	a part; a copy (of a publication)
	部分	Bubun	a part
	大部分	Daibubun	Greater part, most
	本部	Honbu	Headquarters
87.	倍	Bai	Double; times, -fold
	二倍	Nibai	Double, twice as much
	倍にする	Bai ni suru	Double
88.	半	Han, naka(ba)	Half
	半分	Hanbun	Half
	半年	Hantoshi	Half a year, six months
	前半	Zenhan / Zenpan	First half
	大半	Taihan	Greater part, majority
89.	全(く)	Zen, matta(ku)	All, whole, entirely
	全部	Zenbu	All
	全国	Zenkoku	The whole country
	全体	Zentai	The whole, in
	全身	Zenshin	The entire
	万全	Banzen	Perfect, absolutely sure
90.	回	Kai, [E]	Times, repetitions
	回す	Mawasu	Send around, rotate
	回る	Mawaru	Go around, revolve
	十回	Jikkai	Ten times
	今回	Konkai	This time
	前回	Zenkai	Last time
	言い回し	Iimawashi	Expression, turn of phrase
	上回る	Uwamawaru	Be more than, exceed
91.	周(り)	Shū, mawa(ri)	Lap; circumference; surroundings
	一周	Isshū	One lap, one revolution
	半周	Hanshū	Semicircle, halfway around
	円周	Enshū	Circumference

114

	周年	Shūnen	Anniversary
92.	週	Shū	Week
	週間	Shūkan	Week's time
	先週	Senshū	Last week
	今週	Konshū	This week
	来週	Raishū	Next week
	週日	Shūjitsu	Weekday
93.	無(i)	Mu, BU, na(i)	Not be; un-; without, -less
	無名	Mumei	Anonymous; Unknown
	無口	Mukuchi	Taciturn, laconic
	無言	Mugon	Silent, mute
	無休	Mukyū	No holidays, always open
	無事	Buji	Safe and sound
94.	不	Fu, Bu	(prefix) not; un-
	不足	Fusoku	Insufficiency, shortage
	不十分	Fujūbun	Not enough, inadequate
	行方不明	Yukue fumei	Whereabouts unknown, missing
	不当	Futō	improper, unjust
	不死身	Fujimi	Invulnerable
95.	長	Chō, Naga(i)	Long
	部長	Buchō	Department head, director
	身長	Shinchō	Person's height
	長時間	Chōjikan	Long time; many hours
	長年	Naganen	Many years; long years
	長い間	Nagai aida	For a long time
96.	発	Hatsu, Hotsu	Emit; start from; depart
	発明	Hatsumei	Invention
	発見	Hakken	Discovery
	発行	Hakkō	Publish, issue
	出発	Shuppatsu	Departure, start out
	発足	Hossoku, Hassoku	Start, inauguration
97.	心	Shin, kokoro	Heart, mind; core; God, truth
	中心	Chūshin	Center, midpoint
	心身	Shinshin	Mind and body / spirit
	本心	Honshin	One's real mind; real intention
	内心	Naishin	One's innermost heart, true intent
	一心に	Isshin ni	With singlehearted devotion, fervently
98.	性	Sei / Shō	Sex; nature (of) / temperament
	中性	Chūsei	Neuter gender
	性行	Seikō	Character and conduct
	発がん性	Hatsugansei	Carciogenic, cancer-causing
	性分	Shōbun	Nature, temperament
	本性	Honshō, honsei	True nature / character
99.	思	Shi, omo(u)	Think, believe
	思い出	Omoide	Memories
	思い出す	Omoidasu	Remember
	思い切って	Omoikitte	Resolutely, daringly
	思いやり	Omoiyari	Compassion, considerateness
	思い上がった	Omoiagatta	Conceited, cocky
100.	力	Ryoku, Riki, chikara	Force, power
	体力	Tairyoku	Physical Strength
	水力	Suiryoku	Water power, hydraulic power
	風力	Fūryoku	Wind power
	全力	Zenryoku	All one's power, utmost effort
	無力	Muryoku	Powerless, helpless
101.	男	Dan, Nan, otoko	Man, human male
	男性	Dansei	Man; masculine gender
	長男	Chōnan	Eldest son
	男の人	Otokonohito	Man
	山男	Yamaotoko	Mountain dweller; mountaineer
	大男	ōotoko	Giant, tall man

102.	女	Jo, Nyo, [Nyō], onna / me	Woman / feminine
	女性	Josei	Woman; feminine gender
	長女	Chōjo	Eldest daughter
	男女	Danjo	Men and women
	女中	Jochū	Maid
	女の人	Onnanohito	Woman
103.	子	Shi, Su, ko	Child
	男子	Danshi	Boy, man
	男の子	Otokonoko	Boy
	女子	Joshi	Girl, woman
	女の子	Onnanoko	Girl
	分子	Bunshi	Molecule; numerator of a fraction
104.	好	Kō, kono(mu), su(ku)	Like
	好物	Kōbutsu	Favorite food
	好人物	Kōjinnbutsu	Good-natured person
	物好き	Monozuki	Idle curiosity
	大好き	Daisuki	Like very much
	好き好き	Sukizuki	Matter of personal preference
105.	安	An	Peace, peacefulness
	安い	Yasu(i)	Cheap
	安心	Anshin	Feel relieved / reassured
	安全	Anzen	Safety
	不安	Fuan	Unease, anxiety, fear
	目安	Meyasu	Standard, yardstick
	安物	Yasumono	Cheap goods
106.	案	An	Plan, proposal
	案内	Annai	Guidance, information
	案外	Angai	Contrary to expectations
	名案	Meian	Good idea
	思案	Shian	Consideration, reflection
	案出	Anshutsu	Contrive, devise
107.	用	Yō / mochi(iru)	Business; usage / use
	用事	Yōji	Business affair; errand
	用語	Yōgo	(Technical) term, vocabulary
	無用	Muyō	Useless; unnecessary
	男子用	Danshiyō	For men, men's
	用水	Yōsui	City / tap water
108.	電	Den	Electricity
	電力	Denryoku	Electrical power / energy
	電子	Denshi	Electron
	発電	Hatsuden	Generation of electricity
	外電	Gaiden	Telegram from abroad
109.	学	Gaku / mana(bu)	Science, study / Learn
	大学	Daigaku	University, college
	学部	Gakubu	Academic department; faculty
	入学	Nyūgaku	Entry / admission into a school
	学生	Gakusei	Student
	語学	Gogaku	Linguistics
110.	字	Ji / aza	Character, letter / village section
	国字	Kokuji	National / Japanese script
	当て字	Ateji	Kanji used phonetically / for meaning
	ローマ字	Rōmaji	Roman letters
	字体	Jitai	Form of a character / type font
	十字	Jūji	A cross
111.	文	Bun, Mon / fumi	Literature, text, sentence / letter, note
	文字	Moji, monji	Character, letter
	文学	Bungaku	Literature
	本文	Honbun, honmon	Text, wording
	文語	Bungo	Written language
	文明	Bunmei	Civilization

112.	母	Bo, haha	Mother
	母子	Boshi	Mother and child
	生母	Seibo	One's biological mother
	母方	Hahakata	Maternal, on the mother's side
	お母さん	Okaasan	Mother
113.	父	Fu, chichi	Father
	父母	Fubo, chichihaha	Father and mother
	父子	Fushi	Father and child
	父方	Fukata	Fraternal, father's side of the family
	父上	Fuue, Chichiue	Father, male ancestor (polite, pre-Meiji)
	お父さん	Otōsan	Father
114.	交	Kō	Intersection; coming and going
	交(じる)(ざる)	Ma(jiru)(zaru)	Mix (intr)
	交(じえる)(ぜる)	Ma(jieru)(zeru)	Mix (tr)
	交(わる)交う	Maji(waru)	Associate (with)
	交(わす)	Ka(wasu)	Exchange (greetings)
	国交	Kokkō	Diplomatic relations
	外交	Gaikō	Foreign policy, diplomacy
	性交	Seikō	Sexual intercourse
115.	校	Kō	School; (printing) proof
	学校	Gakkō	School
	小学校	Shōgakkō	Elementary school
	中学校	Chūgakkō	Middle school
	母校	Bokō	Alma mater
	校長	Kōchō	Principal, headmaster
116.	毎	Mai	Every, each
	毎年	Mainen, Maitoshi	Every year
	毎月	Maigetsu, Maitsuki	Every month, monthly
	毎週	Maishū	Every week, weekly
	毎日	Mainichi	Every day, daily
	毎時	Maiji	Every hour, hourly
117.	海	Kai, umi	Sea, ocean
	大海	Taikai	An ocean
	海上	Kaijō	Ocean, seagoing, marine
	海外	Kaigai	Overseas, abroad
	内海	Uchiumi, naikai	Inland sea
	日本海	Nihonkai	Sea of Japan
118.	地	Chi, ji	Earth, land
	土地	Toji	Land, soil
	地下	Chika	Underground, subterranean
	地方	Chihō	Region, area
	地名	Chimei	Place name
	生地	Chiji	Material, cloth
119.	池	Chi, ike	Pond
	用水地	Yōsuichi	Water reservoir
	電池	Denchi	Battery
	池田	Ikeda	(Surname)
120.	他	Ta, hoka	Other, another
	他人	Tanin	Another person; stranger
	他国	Takoku	Another / foreign country
	他方	Tahō	The other side / party / direction
	自他	Jita	Oneself and others
	その他	Sonota	And so forth
121.	立	Ritsu, [Ryū], ta(tsu)	Stand (up)
	立(てる)	Tateru	Set up, raise
	国立	Kokuritsu	National, state-supported
	自立	Jiritsu	Independent, self-supporting
	中立	Chūritsu	Neutral, neutrality
	目立つ	Medatsu	Be conspicuous, stick out

	立ち上がる	Tachiagaru	Stand up
122.	位	I, Kurai	Rank, position
	地位	Chii	Rank, position
	学位	Gakui	Academic degree
	上位	Jōi	Higher rank
	本位	Hon'I	Monetary standard, basis, principle
	位取り	Kuraidori	Position (before/after decimal)
123.	法	Hō, ha, ho	Law
	国法	Kokuhō	Laws of the country
	立法	Rippō	Enactment of legislature
	法案	Hōan	Bill, legislative proposal
	文法	Bunpō	Grammar
	方法	Hōhō	Method
124.	和	Wa, [O]	Peace, harmony, (short for Japanese)
	和(らげる)	Yawa(rageru)	Soften, calm down
	和(らぐ) / 和(む)	Yawa(ragu)/nago(mu)	Soften, calm down
	和(やか)	Nagoyaka	Mild, gentle, congenial
	和風	Wafū	Japanese style
	不和	Fuwa	Disharmony, discord, enmity
	大和	Yamato	(old) Japan
125.	私	Shi, watakushi	I; private
	私事	Shiji	Personal affairs
	私物	Shibutsu	Private property
	私用	Shiyō	Private use
	私立	Shiritsu	Private, privately supported
	私自身	Watashi jishin	Personally, as for me
126.	公	Kō, ōyake	Public, official
	公安	Kōan	Public peace / security
	公法	Kōhō	Public law
	公立	Kōritsu	Public
	公海	Kōkai	International waters
	公言	Kōgen	Public declaration, avowal
127.	林	Rin, hayashi	Woods, forest
	山林	Sanrin	Mountains and Forests; mountain forest
	(山)林学	(San)Ringaku	Forestry
	林立	Rinritsu	Stand close together in large numbers
	小林	Kobayashi	(surname)
128.	森	Shin, mori	Woods, forest
	森林	Shinrin	woods, forest
	大森	Ōmori	Area of Tokyo
129.	竹	Chiku, take	Bamboo
	竹林	Chikurin, takebayashi	Bamboo grove / thicket
	竹刀	Shinai	Bamboo sword (kendō)
	さお竹	Saodake	Bamboo pole
	竹のつえ	Take no tsue	Bamboo cane
	竹やぶ	Takeyabu	Bamboo thicket
130.	筆	Hitsu, fude	Writing brush
	万年筆	Mannenfude	Fountain Pen
	自筆	Jihitsu	One's own handwriting
	筆名	Hitsumei	Pen name, pseudonym
	文筆	Bunpitsu	Literary work, writing
	筆先	Fudesaki	Tip of the writing brush
131.	書	Sho, ka(ku)	Write
	書物	Shomotsu	Book
	文書	Bunsho, Monjo	(in)writing, document
	書名	Shomei	Book title
	前書き	Maegaki	Preface, forward
	書き取り	Kakitori	Dictation
132.	意	I	Will, heart, mind,thought;meaning,sense
	意見	Iken	Opinion

	用意	Yōi	Preparations, readiness
	好意	Kōi	Goodwill, good wishes, kindness
	意外	Igai	Unexpected, surprising
	不意	Fui	Sudden, unexpected
133.	車	Sha, kuruma	Vehicle, wheel
	電車	Densha	Electric train
	人力車	Jinrikisha	Rickshaw
	発車	Hassha	Departure
	下車	Gesha	Get off (a train)
	水車	Suishaw	Waterwheel
134.	気	Ki, Ke	Spirit, soul, mood
	人気	Ninki	Popularity
	気分	Kibun	Feeling, mood
	本気	Honki	Seriousness, (in) earnest
	気体	Kitai	A gas
	電気	Denki	Electricity
135.	汽	Ki	Steam
	汽車	Kisha	Steam Train / Locomotive
136.	原	Gen / hara	Original, fundamental / plain, field, wilderness
	原案	Gen'an	The original plan / proposal
	原書	Gensho	(In) the original text
	原文	Genbun	The text, the original
	原生林	Genseirin	Primeval / virgin forest
	原子	Genshi	Atom
137.	元	Gen, Gan, moto	Origin, foundation
	元日	Ganjitsu	New Year's Day
	元金	Gankin	Principal (vs. interest)
	元気	Genki	Healthy, peppy
	地元	Jimoto	Local
138.	光	Kō, hikari / hika(ru)	Light / shine
	日光	Nikkō	Sunlight, sunshine
	月光	Gekkō	Moonlight
	光年	Kōnen	Light-year
	発光	Hakkō	Luminosity, emit light
	電光	Denkō	Electric light, lighting
139.	工	Kō, Ku	Artisan; manufacturing, construction
	工事(中)	Kōji(chū)	Under Construction
	大工	Daiku	Carpenter
	女工	Jokō	Woman factory-worker
	工学	Kōgaku	Engineering
	人工	Jinkō	Man-made, artificial
140.	空	Kū, sora / a(keru/ku)/ kara	Sky / make, (be unoccupied) / empty
	空気	Kūki	Air
	時間と空間	Jikan to Kūkan	Time and Space
	空車	Kūsha	Empty car, for hire (taxi)
	空手	Karate	empty-handed; karate
	大空	Ōzora	Sky, firmament
141.	天	Ten, ame, [ama]	Heaven
	天気	Tenki	Weather
	天文学	Tenmongaku	Astronomy
	天国	Tengoku	Paradise
	天性	Tensei	Nature, natural constitution
	天の川	Amanogawa	Milky Way
142.	里	Ri / sato	(old unit of length: 2.9km) / village, one's Parent's home
	千里	Senri	1,000ri; a great distance
	海里	Kairi	Nautical mile
	里子	Satogo	Foster child
	里心	Satogokoro	Homesickness

143.	理	Ri	Reason, logic, principle
	地理学	Chirigaku	Geography
	心理学	Shinrigaku	Psychology
	理学部	Rigakubu	Department of Science
	無理	Muri	Unreasonable; impossible; (by) force
	理事	Riji	Director
144.	少	Shō, suko(shi) / suku(nai)	A little / little, few, slight
	少年	Shōnen	Boy
	少年法	Shōnenhō	The Juvenile Law
	少女	Shōjo	Girl
	少々	Shōshō	A little
	少しずつ	Sukoshizutsu	Little by little, a little at a time
145.	省	Sei, kaeri(miru) / Shō / habu(ku)	Reflect upon, give heed to
	自省	Jisei	reflection, introspection
	内省	Naisei	Introspection
	人事不省	Jinjifusei	Unconsciousness, fainting
	文部省	Monbushō	Ministry of Education
146.	相	Sō / Shō / ai	Aspect, phase / (gov) minister / together
	相当	Sōtō	Suitable, appropriate
	文相	Bunshō	Minister of Education
	外相	Gaishō	Foreign Minister
	相手	Aite	The other party, partner, opponent
147.	想	Sō, [so]	Idea, thought
	思想	Shisō	Idea, thought
	回想	Kaisō	Retrospection, reminiscence
	理想	Risō	An ideal
	空想	Kūsō	Fantasy, daydream
	めい想	Meisō	Meditation
148.	首	Shu, kubi	Neck, head
	首相	Shushō	Prime Minister
	元首	Genshu	Sovereign, ruler
	首位	Shui	Leading position, top spot
	部首	Bushu	Radical of a kanji
	手首	Tekubi	Wrist
149.	道	Dō, [Tō], michi	Street, way, path
	国道	Kokudō	National highway
	水道	Suidō	Water conduits, running water
	北海道	Hokkaidō	Hokkaido
	書道	Shodō	Calligraphy
	回り道	Mawarimichi	A detour
150.	通	Tsū, [Tsu], tō(ru)(su) / kayo(u)	go through, pass, let through, commute
	交通	Kōtsū	Traffic, transportation
	文通	Buntsū	Correspondence, exchange of letters
	通学	Tsūgaku	Attend school
	見通し	Mitōshi	Prospects, outlook
151.	路	Ro, -ji	Street way
	道路	Dōro	Street, road
	十字路	Jūjiro	Intersection, crossroads
	水路	Suiro	Waterway, aqueduct
	海路	Kairo	Sea route
	通路	Tsūro	Passageway, walkway, aisle
152.	戸	Ko, to	Door
	戸外で	Kogai de	Outdoors, in the open air
	下戸	Geko	Nondrinker, teetotaler
	戸口	Toguchi	Doorway
	木戸	Kido	Gate, entrance; castle gate
	雨戸	Amado	Storm door, shutter
153.	所	Sho, tokoro	Place
	案内所	Annaijo	Inquiry office, information desk
	名所	Meisho	Noted place, sights (to see)
	所長	Shochō	Director, head, manager

	長所	Chōsho	Strong point, merit, advantage
	原子力発電所	Genshiryoku Hatsudensho	Nuclear power plant
154.	場	Jō, ba	Place
	工場	Kōjō, kōba	Factory, plant
	出場	Shutsujō	Stage appearance, participation
	場所	Basho	Place, location
	立場	Tachiba	standpoint, point of view
	相場	Sōba	Market Price
155.	主	Shu, [su], nushi / omo	Lord, master, main / main, principal
	主人	Shujin	Husband, head of household
	主人公	Shujinkō	Hero, main character
	自主	Jishu	Independence, autonomy
	主語	Shugo	Subject (in grammar)
	地主	Jinushi	Landowner, landlord
156.	住	Jū, su(mu), su(mau)	Live, dwell, reside
	住所	Jūsho	An address
	住人	Jūnin	Peaceful living
	住まい	Sumai	Residence, where one lives, address
	住み心地	Sumigokochi	Confortableness, liveability
157.	信	Shin	Faith, trust, believe
	信用	Shinyō	Trust
	不信	Fushin	bad faith, insincerity; distrust
	自信	Jishin	Self confidence
	所信	Shoshin	One's conviction, opinion
	通信	Shūshin	Communication, correspondence
158.	会	Kai / E, a(u)	Meeting; association / meet
	国会	Kokkai	Parliament, diet, congress
	大会	Taikai	Mass meeting, sports meet, (Tournament)
	学会	Gakkai	Learned / academic society
	会見	Kaiken	Interview, news conference
	出会う	Deau	Happen to meet, run into, encounter
159.	合	Ai, Gō,Ga,[Ka],a(u)/a(waseru)/a(wasu)	Harmony / Fit / put together
	合意	Gōi	Mutual consent, agreement
	場合	Baai, bawai	(in this) case
	お見合い	Omiai	Marriage interview
	間に合う	Maniau	Be in time (for); will do, suffice
	見合わせる	Miawaseru	Look at each other; postpone
160.	答	Tō, kota(e) / kotaeru	An answer / answer
	回答	Kaitō	An answer, reply
	口答	Kōtō	Oral answer
	筆答	Hittō	Written answer
	名答	Meitō	Correct answer
	答案	Tōan	Examination paper
161.	門	Mon, kado	Gate
	入門（書）	Nyūmon(sho)	Introduction, primer
	部門	Bumon	Group, category, branch
	名門	Meimon	Distinguished / illustrious family
	門下生	Monkasei	(someone's) pupil
	門口	Kadoguchi	Front door, entrance

Index

Aikido 合氣道 (Way of Spiritual Harmony), 5, 11, 28-29, 34-35, 71, 102

Ai 愛 (love) *kanji* calligraphy, 94

AiShin 合心 (Harmonious Heart) *kanji* calligraphy, 93

AiShinKai 合心会 (Harmonious Heart Association), 5, 8, 11, 18-20, 23, 31, 75

AiShin-Ryu Aikido 合心流合氣道 (Harmonious Heart Style Way of Spiritual Harmony), 11

All Japan Kendo Federation (*Zen Nihon Kendo Renmei* 全日本剣道連盟), 29

Aku-Sen-Ku-Tou 悪戦苦闘 (Struggle Hard Against Wrong-Doing) four-character idiom, 85

An-Shin-Ritsu Mei 安心立命 (Religious Enlightenment), four-character idiom, 83

archery, 29, 31, 73

"barb" basic stroke #6 (dot), 49

Basic Principles of *Shodo*, 23, 25-34, 41

basic strokes, 16, 36, 41-57

basic stroke 1: horizontal line (*yokoga* 横画) "bone" or "bamboo", 42, 45

basic strokes #2,#3,#4: vertical lines (*tageta* 縦画), 43, 47

basic strokes #5, #6: Dots "raindrop" and "barb" (*ten* 点), 49

basic stroke #7: "long sword" (*katana* 刀), 51

basic stroke #8: "short sword" (*kodachi* 小太刀), 51

basic stroke #9: "collar" (*kesa* 袈裟), 53

basic stroke #10: "dragon claw" (*Ryuu no Tsume* 龍の爪), 53

basic stroke #11: "*hera* 篦 (spatula) or "slide", 55

basic stroke #12: continuous line (*tensetsu* 転折) "fishhook", 57

blank worksheet, 87

Block script (*Kaisho*), 14, 15, 19, 36, 59, 63, 69, 71, 73

bokujuu 墨汁 (prepared ink), 21

"bone" or "bamboo" basic stroke 1: horizontal line (*yokoga*), 42, 45

Bonsai, 14

Breathing and Meditation Exercises, 24-25, 31

brush, brushes (*fude* 筆), 13, 17, 22, 23

brush rest (*fudeoki* 筆置), 17, 23

Budo 武道 (martial arts; Way of Warriors), 77

Bun-Bu-Ryodo 文武両道 (classics and sword are one), 11, 28-30, 34-35

bunchin (paper weight), 17, 23

Bunsho, Kasumi 春見文勝, "Tranquil Wisdom Sword (静恵剣)" *kakejiki* scroll calligraphy, 95

Bu-Shin 武心 (Masaaki Hatsumi), 34

Business Leadership, 5, 7-8, 13-14, 18-20

calligraphy pad (*shitajiki* 下敷), 17, 23

Calmness, 5, 7-8, 16, 23, 24, 25, 41

children, 13, 36, 89

Clerical script (*Reisho* 隷書), 14, 15

"collar" (*kesa* 袈裟) basic stroke #9, 53

composition, 31-33, 41, 59-67, 69-77, 81-85

Conflict Resolution, 13, 18-20

Confucianism, 13

cursive style (*Sosho* 草書), 14, 15

dango 団子 (dumpling), 22, 42, 47

Do 道 (Way) *kanji*, 63, 65, 67

Dots 点 (*ten*) basic strokes #5 and #6, 47

"dragon claw" (*Ryuu no Tsume* 龍の爪) basic stroke #10, 53

Eastern *Jin* dynasty, 13

Ei 永 (forever) *kanji*, 59

enso 円相 (circle), 79

Eura Kazunori, 5, 28-29, 35

four-character ideom, 81-85

Four Treasures, 13, 17, 23

fude 筆 (brush), 17, 22, 23

Fude Kuyo 筆供養 (brush memorial service), 17

fudeoki 筆置 (brush rest), 17, 23

"Good For Kids Too . . ." *kanji* worksheet, 89

Gyokko of Hoen-ji, "Dragon (*Ryuu* 龍)" *kakejiki* scroll calligraphy, 96

Gyosho 行書 (semi-cursive script), 14, 15, 19, 36, 61, 65, 75, 77

Han dynasty, 15

Harmonious Heart Association (*AiShinKai* 合心会), 13

HaruIchiban 春一番 (Spring is Best) *kanji* calligraphy, 94

hassetsu 八節 (eight movements of Kyudo), Heian period (*Heian Jidai* 平安時代), 13

"*hera*" 篦 (spatula) basic stroke #11, 55

hiragana (平仮名), 16

horizontal lines (*yokoga* 横画), 42, 45

Iaido 居合道, 5, 13, 28-29, 35, 69

ideogrammatic characters, 14

Ikebana 生け花 (living flowers), 14

ink (*sumi* 墨), 13, 17, 21

ink stone (*suzuri* 硯), 17, 21

ink well "ocean" (*umi* 海), 17, 21, 30, 42, 43

inochi-ge 命毛 (core brush bristles), 31

Iwata Norikazu, "*Zen Hen Shi Yu*," *kakejiku* calligraphy, 100

Kaa-Fou-Chou-Getsu 花鳥風月 (The Beauties of Nature: flowers, birds, wind moon) four-character idiom, 81

Kaisho 楷書 (block script), 14, 15, 19, 36, 59, 63, 69, 71, 73

kakejiku 掛物 (hanging scroll), 32, 69-77

kami 紙 (paper), 17

kanji 漢字 (Chinese characters), 14-16, 36, 59-67, 69-85, 108-120 (index)
kasure 掠れ (scratching), 21, 33
katakana 片仮名, 16
"*katana*" 刀 (long sword) basic stroke #7, 51
"*kesa*" 袈裟 (collar) basic stroke #9, 53
Ki 氣 (spiritual power), 27, 28, 94, 102
Ki 氣 (spiritual power) *kanji* calligraphy, 94, 102
Ki-Ken-Tai-Ichi 気剣体一 (spirit-sword-body-one), 29
kirioroshi 切り下ろし (downward slash), 43
"*kodachi*" 小太刀 (short sword) basic stroke #8, 51
Kokikai International, 5
Kun, Feri (calligrapher), 61
Kyudo 弓道, 13, 29, 73

land (ink grinding area on stone "*riku* 陸 "), 17, 21, 30, 42-43
leadership, 5, 7-8, 13-14, 18-20, 28-29
line weight, 33
literacy, 13

martial arts, 5, 7-8, 13, 19-20, 24, 28-29, 34-35
Maruyama Shuji, 5, 34
Masaaki Hatsumi 初見良昭 "*Bu-Shin* 武心 (Warrior Mind)", 34
Meiji Restoration, 13
Menjyo 免許, *AiShinKai* grade certificate, author's calligraphy, 101
Michi 道, 67
Mind-Body Coordination Exercises, 8, 25-26, 41
MuShin 無心 (No Mind) *kanji* calligraphy, 94

Nature, 30
najimi 滲み (blotting), 21, 33
nukitsuke 抜付 (sword drawing), 28

Pacific Northwest Budo Association, 5
paper(s), 13, 22
paperweight (*bunchin* 文鎮), 17
phonetic symbols, 14
pictographs, 14
Pikachu, 89
posture, 23, 24, 25, 26, 27, 30, 31, 41, 69

Qin dynasty, 15
"raindrop" basic stroke #5 (dot), 47

Reisho 隷書 (clerical script), 14, 15
relaxation, 8, 16, 23, 24, 25, 41
rhythm, 30, 31, 42-43
riku 陸 (grinding area "land"), 17, 30, 42, 43
"*Ryuu no Tsume*" 龍の爪 (dragon claw) basic stroke #10, 53

samurai 侍, 13
Seal script (*Tensho* 篆書), 14, 15
self-mastery, 5, 13, 16, 18, 23, 36
Sekiguchi, Kenji 関口剣志, "*Shisei* 至誠 (Sincerity)", 97
semi-cursive script (*Gyosho* 行書), 14, 15

Shibayama Zenkei 柴山全慶 "*Enso* 円相 (circle)," 98
shitajiki 下敷 (calligraphy pad), 17
Sho 書 (writing) *kanji*, 61
Shoko Hirose, "*Ryuu* 龍 (Dragon)," 96, 99
shu-ha-ri 守破離 (hold, break, leave), 19-20
size (of characters), 32
"slide" (*tensetsu* 転折) basic stroke #12, 57
Soseki, Muso 夢窓疎石, "No Spiritual Meaning (別無工夫)" *kakejiki* scroll calligraphy, 95
Sosho 草書 (cursive script), 14, 15, 20, 36, 67
"spatula" 箆 (*hera*) basic stroke #11, 55
stones, for ink (*suzuri* 硯), 13
stop-start-stop (*ton-dou-ton* 遯動遯), 15, 30, 42, 43
stroke order, 30, 59
stroke weight, 33
sumi 墨 (ink), 17, 21
sumioke 墨置 (ink stick rest), 17
Suzuri (硯), 13, 21

Tang dynasty, 15
Tao 道 (Way - *Chinese pronunciation*), 67
tatega 縦画- basic strokes #2,#3,#4 (vertical lines), 43, 47
Team Management, 14, 18-20
Ten 点 (Dots - basic strokes #5 and #6), 49
tensetsu 転折 - continuous line "fishhook", 57
Tensho 篆書 (seal script), 14, 15
Tesshu Koho (*Yamaoka Tesshu* 山岡鉄舟) "Fragrant Grass has Passion, 96
ton-dou-ton 遯動遯 (stop-move-stop), 15, 28, 30, 42, 43
Trent, Don Yoshimoto, 5
Tsubomi Seishin Kan Iaido Kai, 5

Ueshiba, Morihei 植芝盛平, 71
umi 海 (ink well "ocean"), 17, 30, 42, 43
urauchi 裏打 (wetting and backing), 21, 22

vertical lines (*tatega* 縦画), 43

washi 和紙 (paper), 17, 22
water vessel (*suiteki* 水滴), 17

yokoga 横画 (horizontal lines), 42, 45
Yamada, Mumon (*Ensō* 円相), 79

zanshin 残心 (continuous awareness), 28
Zen Buddhism 禅, 79, 95, 96, 98
Zen Hen Shi Yu (*kakejiku* calligraphy by *Iwata Norikazu*), 100

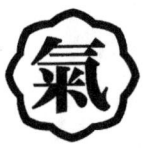